art, lies and videotape:
exposing performance

1 Bill Shannon *The Phenomena of Projected Narrative* (sequential), from *Regarding The Fall* performance series 2003

contents

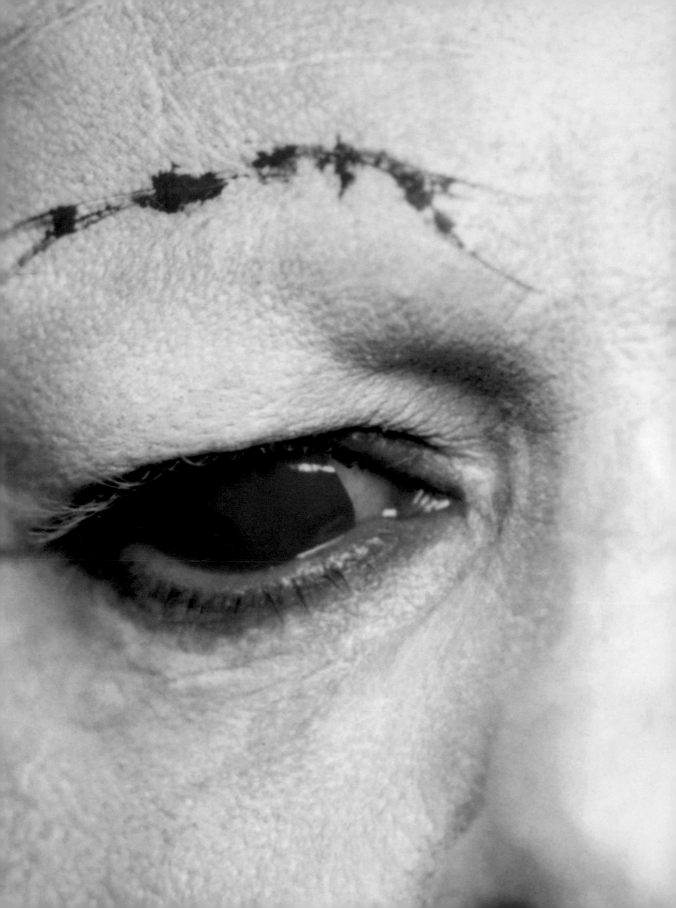

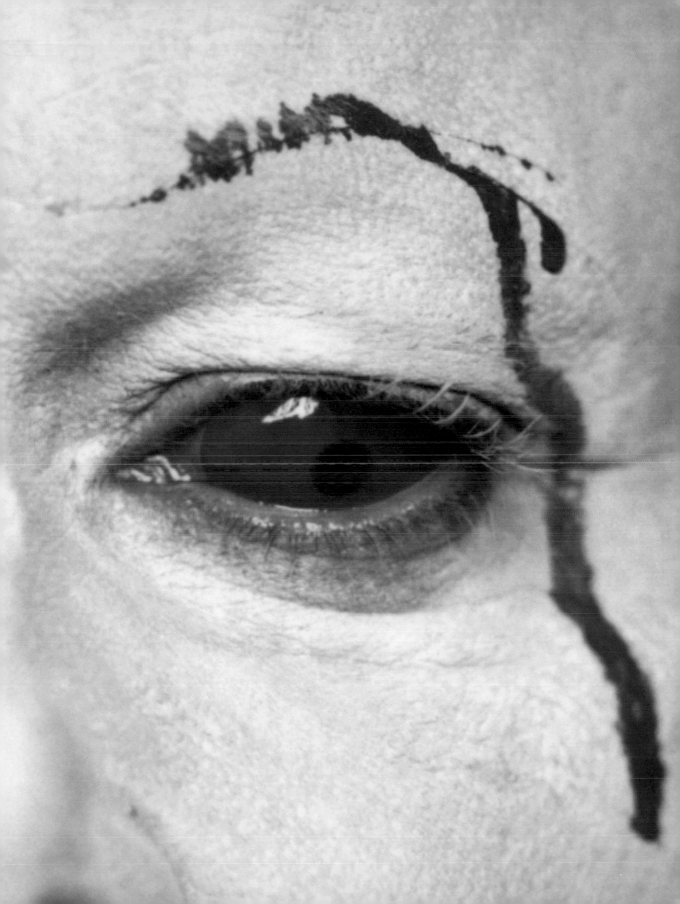

Our sincere thanks go to the following
for their invaluable help with organising this exhibition

Vito Acconci and Mike Bellon, Acconci Studio

Royce Howes, Robert Miller Gallery and John Pelosi,
Diane Arbus Estate

Caroline Tisdall and Ute Klophaus

Trisha Brown and Michele Thompson, Trisha Brown
Dance Company
Angela Choon and Hannah Schouwink, David Zwirner;
Kirk Radke

Chris Burden and Katy Lucas; Sarah Taggart;
Helen Molesworth, Wexner Center for the Arts

Meg Perlman, The Pierre Noel Matissse Trust;
Jacqueline Matisse Monnier

Sheree Rose; Robert J. Shiffler Foundation; Lisa
Melandri, Santa Monica Museum of Art; Melanie
Franklin, New Museum of Contemporary Art; Karen
Alexander and Christine Whitehouse, bfi.

Patrick Bensard and Virginie Aubry, Cinématèque de la
Danse; Adrien Sina

Roberta Cremoncini and Chris Adams, Estorick
Collection of Modern Italian Art; Steven Conor

Dan Graham; Karina Daskalov, Marian Goodman
Gallery; Jean-Michel Bouhours, Isabelle Daire and
Natalie Leleu, Musée National d'Art Modern, Centre
National d'Art et de Culture Georges Pompidou

Philippe Siauve, Yves Klein Archives; Christopher
Eamon, Kramlich Foundation

Robert Longo; Tom Heman, Metro Pictures, New York;
Ben Cook, The Lux; Stephen Vitiello, The Kitchen

Emmanuelle de l'Ecotais, Musée d'Art Moderne de la
Ville de Paris; Camillo d'Afflito

Barbara Moore, Bound and Unbound

Catherine Opie; Sheri Pasquarella, Gorney Bravin &
Lee; Lisa Overduin, Regen Projects; Ron Athey

Antoine Cochet, Pathé International

Robert Rauschenberg, Thomas Buehler, David White,
Robert Rauschenberg Studio; Caroline Brown; Alex Hay

C. Raman Schlemmer, Oskar Schlemmer Theatre Estate;
Bundes Archiv, Berlin

Angela Westwater, Karen Polack, Sperone Westwater,
New York

Felicity Coupland, Gagosian Gallery, London and
Alexandra Batsford, Pace/Macgill Gallery, New York

Franca di Veroli and Nick Radclyffe, Exhibition
Designers

Art, Lies and Videotape: Exposing Performance is Tate's first major exhibition devoted to the history and continuing significance of this radical art form. It presents the history of performance or live art as a complex construction between fact and fiction – of spectacular events never recorded and iconic performances staged exclusively for the camera. Tate Liverpool, along with other arts organisations across the city, has long supported live art through several notable projects. One of the first 'happenings' in England (then described as a 'mixed media event') was staged in 1962 by Adrian Henri at the Merseyside Arts Festival in Liverpool. The Bluecoat Art Centre was one of a few locations in the world to present Yoko Ono's infamous performance *Cut Piece* in 1967 and we are glad to collaborate again with the Bluecoat on a live art programme complementing this exhibition. In 1986, two years before the Tate Gallery in Liverpool opened, *Song for the North* by Bruce McLean and David Ward was commissioned and staged in association with the Walker Art Gallery – an epic performance that brought together singers, water jets and spotlights reverberating of the walls of the Albert Dock. More recently, for the 2002 Liverpool Biennial, Tate Liverpool played host to Jason Rhoades' extraordinary *Pea-Roe-Formance*, a spectacle that saw the top floor galleries filled with irreverent activity and material excess. Bearing such instances in mind, one observes that performance art resonates strongly not only with the local art community but with the city's population in general. Perhaps this can be attributed to a local culture that is defiantly extrovert and deeply performance-orientated, prominently manifested in the city's rich tradition in music, theatre, literature and the visual arts.

Performance art is a transitory medium, resisting presentation within the spatial and temporal confines of an exhibition. Adrian George, Curator at Tate Liverpool, faced this challenge with his usual energy, bringing together a remarkable selection of objects, installations, photographs, films and videos spanning the last century. This would not have been possible without the generosity of the lenders to this show, who not only parted with objects but also helped to reconstruct works, locate lost documents and reprint unseen documentary photographs. Special thanks must also go to the exhibition team at Tate Liverpool who supported the realisation of *Art, Lies and Videotape*, in particular research assistants Cressida Kocienski and Anna Lythgoe, and Education Curator Naomi Horlock, who has realised an excellent events programme to complement this exhibition. As ever, I am grateful to all staff at Tate Liverpool who always set high standards of professionalism for our exhibitions.

For this catalogue, edited by Adrian George, Tate Liverpool is deeply indebted to the authors for enhancing *Art, Lies and Videotape* with such finesse and scholarship: RoseLee Goldberg; Jean-Paul Martinon; Alice Maude-Roxby; Andrew Quick; Tracey Warr; and Aaron Williamson. I would finally like to thank the catalogue production team, Claire Young, Helen Tookey and Jemima Pyne at Tate Liverpool and Piccia Neri for her thoughtful and imaginative catalogue design.

preface

art, lies and videotape: exposing performance

adrian george

'dance',

'theatre', 'happenings', 'actions', 'performance' and many other names can be and have been applied to an entire spectrum of work by artists who have created live art events. An all-encompassing definition is almost impossible, but to put it at its simplest, live art contains a living element, a human presence – a body (or bodies) in space and at a specific moment, or for a definite period. However, it becomes very complicated when historians try to categorise and pigeonhole such a diversity of work. Take an installation that requires a human presence to activate or complete it – could this be defined as a performance? If the work is staged, with a set and recognisable movements – is that theatre or dance, or is it performance art? Does wearing a swan costume make it ballet and performing naked make it live art? These are just some of the many difficulties encountered when trying to discuss such actions.

The very fact that it is difficult to name makes this medium inherently subversive and perhaps that is why live art has always been the playground of the radical. The Italian Futurists, a group of artists, writers and musicians whose work, at the beginning of the twentieth century, caused great public outcry, chose performance as one of their modes of communication. Many artists who have felt marginalised have turned to performance as a means of political as well as artistic comment – feminists of the '60s and '70s seeking to combat what was a male-dominated art market; lesbian and gay art activists of the '80s and '90s trying to educate people about, as well as cope with, the outbreak of HIV/AIDS; and black and disabled artists to this day who use their bodies to extraordinary visual effect to communicate their unique perspectives on contemporary culture.

There is an almost irresistible and unconscious urge to name, categorise and collate built into every art historian and curator. It is precisely for this reason that many artists have felt driven to create work that denies or even defies classification. For many, the main subversive strategy is to create a non-object-based arts practice. Many artists, whose work has become part of Conceptual art history, could quite easily have been reconfigured as performance artists. For instance, Manzoni's *Body of Air n. 28 (Corpo d'aria)* 1960 (Fig. 1), often cited as an early Conceptual work, is quite clearly the object-remnant of an action: the artist blew up a balloon that slowly deflated over time. If we reflect on the action, rather than the concept or the remnant, then this becomes a performance. Even though the focus for the true Conceptual artist was the idea or process, the results are, whether by chance or intention, highly exhibitable written statements, proposals, photographs – even maps, films and objects.

Other artists are often connected tangentially with performance. Jackson Pollock, for example, is often termed an 'action painter' because of the physicality of his painting technique. His aim, though, was to create a painting rather than to stage an event. Many performance artists have no intention of making any sort of object but nevertheless feel driven to create some record of their actions – often through the media of photography, film or video, and in some cases by presenting remnants of objects left by or created during a performance. These docu-

Fig. 1
Piero Manzoni
Body of Air n. 28 1960

art, lies and videotape: exposing performance

ments are then used to promote or represent the performance, to position the work within a historical context and, in some cases, to act as limited editions available for sale.

This is where *Art, Lies and Videotape* begins. I have chosen to look at performance from the perspective of the document. However, performance documents are not without their associated problems. Tracing back in time means that documents are few. At the end of the nineteenth century photography, sound recording and film were still in their infancy, so what documents remain from this period are rare. RoseLee Goldberg's book *Performance Art: From Futurism to the Present* (Thames and Hudson, 1979) came to my attention in my first year of art

4
Peter Moore, *John Lennon and Yoko Ono performing at Ken Dewey Memorial* 1972

school. The history it explores, the art and artists it describes, have fascinated me ever since. Without doubt Goldberg's research into the many stories of performance broke new ground in terms of the history of art and it was without hesitation that I approached her to write about the section of this exhibition titled *Lost Histories*. Having been instrumental in disclosing the many overlooked performance works by some of the best known artists today Goldberg is perfectly placed to comment on history's failure when there is quite simply nothing to archive.

In recent years there has been a renewed interest in performance and with this a plethora of new publications that present many photographs from the history of live art. However, these static images do not record the duration of a performance, or the sounds, smells or even temperature of the venue or location, yet in many instances such images have come to represent an entire performance and the same image is printed every time that specific performance is discussed. Tracey Warr, in her role as editor of *The Artist's Body* (Phaidon, 2000), had the difficult task of deciding whether to include in her publication the famous photographs or to search out less well-known images. I could think of no one better to write on the difficult issue of the *Image as Icon*.

When an image becomes invaluable as the only record of a performance it suddenly seems obvious that artists would seek to challenge the viewer on this very issue. There are many images of actions so extreme that it is almost impossible to believe that the event took place – Rudolf Schwarzkogler's rumoured self-castration perhaps, or Yves Klein's life-threatening leap from a high gatepost. Both are, of course, fakes – more accurately, one staged for the camera and the other a photomontage. There are many performance artists who actually put their bodies through extreme suffering, almost to the point of unbearable pain. One has to ask: why do they push/punish themselves to this extent when it is perfectly possible to fake it? These are questions that Jean-Paul Martinon addresses in his essay *Fact or Fiction*.

The boulevards of Paris and seaside promenades, fashionable at the beginning of the twentieth century, literally made catwalks for the rich and beautiful. With the advent of CCTV it is even more evident today that we are all 'on show' when in public. For many disabled people, whether their bodies are used in art-making or not, the problems they encounter in simply trying to function in a society designed for the able-bodied become 'performative events'. *The Unconscious Performance* looks at those artists who implicate or incorporate unwitting members of the public in their work. Aaron Williamson discusses whether a performance can be invisible or unconscious but also questions the use of images of disabled people in art – are these subjects aware of how they will be finally presented?

As Tracey Warr mentions, the photograph, above all other media, has become crucial in the historicisation of performance. However, it is not such an easy thing to create a good document. Babette Mangolte, one of the most successful performance photographers working on the New York arts scene of the 1970s, suggests that an empathic bond, a creative link between the artist and the photographer, is essential. Focusing on the often highly creative, sometimes very difficult relationship between the artist and the person who documents his or her work, Alice Maude-Roxby writes on the section of the exhibition *Me and My Camera(person)*.

With so much emphasis now on the documentation of work, why should performance artists make the effort of staging actual performances? Many Fluxus artists, for instance, wrote instructions that members of the public could act out, in effect directing

14

5
Joseph Beuys
*I Like America
and America Likes Me* 1972

others to perform for them. Artists such as Dennis Oppenheim or Tony Oursler have created stand-ins, mannequins or puppets that perform on command, while other artists have become filmmakers, some even taking this to Hollywood. In the section *The Artist as Director* Andrew Quick looks at why performance artists still perform when a film of their work could reach a much wider (possibly global) audience. — maybe they don't want to

The visual arts are considered to be the breeding ground for ideas that push culture and society forward to greater invention, discovery and achievement. Performance is seen to be the 'avant avant-garde' (Abramovic, 2003[1]). The advent of reality TV identifies the public fascination with what is happening here and now, with the moment, with the real. In tandem with this there is a growing interest across the world in performance and live art, with conferences, projects and increasingly exhibitions devoted to the subject.

Art, Lies and Videotape: Exposing Performance is not a chronology and is not a survey. I have had to make some very difficult decisions about which work to incorporate. There are many names and many items I wish I could have included and I'm sure there are many more artists who remain unknown to me. However, this exhibition looks at some important issues and key moments across many performance art histories and

Fig. 2
Luigi Russolo
Instruments used in the
'Grand Futurist Concert of Noises'
at the London Coliseum
'Noise-Tuners' rehearsing 1913

15

1 Marina Abramovic 'Live Culture', lecture given at Tate Modern, London, 29 March 2003

in so doing presents reconstructions and original artworks along-side what can only be termed a vast array of extraordinary performance documents.

It would be frustrating to present so many images that reference the live event without presenting the live event itself, so this exhibition is accompanied by a programme of performance at the Bluecoat Arts Centre as well as a series of education events presented at Tate Liverpool. In addition to the regular in-gallery education programmes we are hosting a one-day *Imaging the Body* seminar, in conjunction with the North West Disability Arts Forum, and a conference in association with Liverpool University, the papers from which will be published. We will also present a unique meeting of minds with RoseLee Goldberg in conversation with Babette Mangolte.

To bring this extensive project to fruition in such a short time would have been impossible without the support of many people. I would like to thank all the artists and lenders for their generosity in offering works to this exhibition – many at very short notice. In the planning stages of this project I sought advice from Donna De Salvo, RoseLee Goldberg, Jon Hendricks, Babette Mangolte and Barbara Moore, whose knowledge and insight have been invaluable. Lois Keidan and Daniel Brine at the Live Art Development Agency, London have been on call, as has Adrien Sina, who recommended many works for the film programme presented in the gallery foyer. From institutions across the world many have gone to great lengths to assist me and in particular I would like to thank: Helen Cole at Arnolfini, Bristol; Ben Cook, Lux, London; Jean-Michel Bouhours, Isabelle Daire and Nathalie Leleu at Centre National d'Art Contemporain Georges Pompidou, Paris; and Helen Molesworth at The Wexner Center for the Arts, Ohio. Finally I would like to thank the catalogue authors for their amazing contributions to this book and the research assistants and teams at Tate, specifically at Tate Liverpool, without whom this exhibition could not take place.

6
Martin Scorsese
The Big Shave 1963

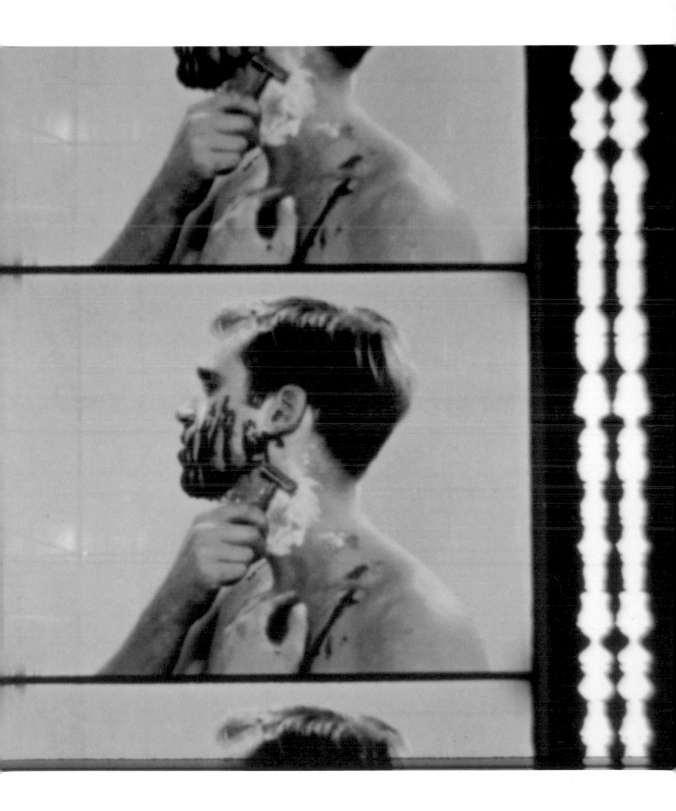

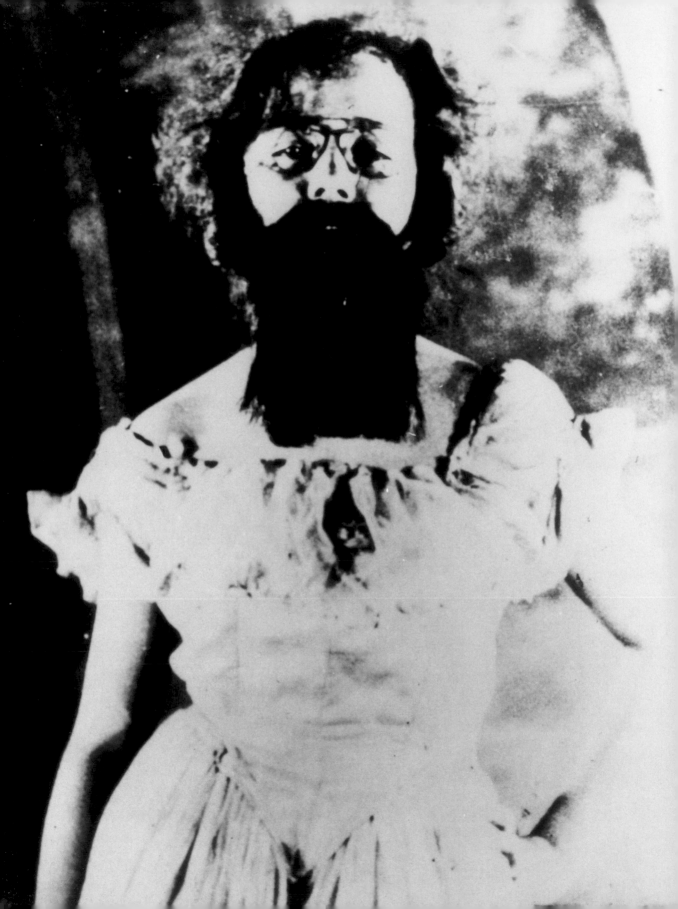

lost histories

René Clair
Interval 1924
Film still photograph of Francis Picabia

hidden from history: performance art and the imagination

roselee goldberg

watch closely how culture and politics, power and glory of today are continuously shifting, and it is easy to understand how certain events become lost in the untidy chronicle of passing time. Performance art, until the late 1970s, was hidden from history, not because of any deliberate omission, but because it fitted no category. Art historians, trained to collate visual clues with solid evidence to back their observations, seemed not to know how to categorise live performances by artists or the scattered ephemera they left behind, especially when many artists' actions deliberately confused and refuted the very practices of their profession. Once uncovered, however, the importance of such events opened art history to unexpected, even radical revisions, forever changing the course of well established art history studies.

Artists who created performances, whether Italian Futurists in the early decades of the twentieth century, or Fluxus artists later on, did so because they took pleasure in avoiding categories alto-

Oskar Schlemmer
The Triadic Ballet 1922

Left to right:
8 *The Disc*
9 *The Spiral*
10 *The Diver*

21

gether. They sashayed between disciplines, lifting elements from one or the other as they pleased, to create unusual combinations: sound poetry recited on a stage hung with paintings, a dance of swirling lights performed to the sound of noise instruments, a week-long drama of a man and a coyote installed in a gallery as a metaphorical meditation on the nature of colonial exploitation. In doing so they expressed a broad fascination with the social, aesthetic or political matrix that held their various worlds together, insisting that the role of the artist extend well beyond the making of singular objects. Interaction or collaboration with individuals trained in other disciplines – poets, composers, architects – brought entirely new points of view to the visual art world, as well as people from a range of fields seeking a permissive environment for untried ideas in their chosen area.

This meeting-place of unusual minds – be it in a café in Milan, in Zürich or in New York – where ideas were fermented and from where actions fanned out to intimate theatres such as the Salle Gaveau in 1920s Paris, innovative art schools such as the Bauhaus in Germany after the First World War and Black Mountain College in the United States after the Second, or the lofts and 'alternative spaces' of downtown Manhattan in the 1960s and 1970s, often shaped the aesthetics and form of the 'solid' arts, painting or sculpture. The full range of debate, of conceptual methods and intrapersonal influences on the genesis of a painting or a sculpture, could often be found in earlier performed actions. Performance, because it is ephemeral and in its early history was mostly executed by artists in the first decade of their careers, seemed to invite

hidden from history: performance art and the imagination

11
Loïe Fuller
Untitled c 1905

12
Robert Rauschenberg
and John Cage
Automobile Tire Print 1953
(detail)

artists to be as radical and as provocative as they possibly could be. Events such as an installation at the first European Dada fair in 1920, hung with paintings, photographs and life-size dummies, or a performance with Merce Cunningham, John Cage, David Tudor, Robert Rauschenberg and other students in North Carolina in the summer of 1952 that included a concert on a 'prepared piano' and film projections on the ceiling, triggered new ideas about space, about materiality, about chance. It is the spontaneity and inventiveness of these collective actions that most often provides clues for the historian attempting to analyse aesthetic considerations among a circle of Berlin or New York artists in the years immediately following such lively interactions.

Given the critical role of performance in the history of twentieth-century art, and its now accepted and generally well-documented place in the opening years of the twenty-first, the task for the art historians covering performance is a demanding one because, as the artists themselves do, these writers must cover a spectrum of disciplines. They must also delve deep into the history of each discipline to understand the ignition that occurs when two distinct surfaces connect: the edge where visual art meets dance or music or film history is where such historians must tread. To fully grasp, for example, the radical nature of choreographers Yvonne Rainer or Trisha Brown and the influential Judson Group which they and others formed, a knowledge of milestones in dance history from Loïe Fuller (3, 11) to Ruth St Denis, Isadora Duncan, Martha Graham, Anna Halprin and Cunningham is essential, as is information on the choreographers' relationship to artists Robert Morris, Robert Rauschenberg or Carolee Schneemann; an understanding of anti-Vietnam politics and student, feminist and civil rights activism; and, not least, a knowledge of the economic conditions governing real estate markets which made the large church

hall (where Judson gathered) and similarly sized industrial spaces available for open-ended, improvisatory performances.

Performance art history calls for just such a rounded, 'contextual' approach. Also referred to as 'the sociology of art', analysis of this kind gradually unravels the layers of motives and meaning behind actions and art product. It also provides a glimpse of the audience, so that the sociology of the art world is under the spotlight too. Interaction with a public – whether of the *épater les bourgeois* kind, intended to shock, or among intimate circles of artists, lovers, friends and interested followers – has always been a goal of performance. Though drawn by general public announcements, the audiences who gathered at the Teatro Costanzi in Rome in March 1913 to hear and see Filippo Tommaso Marinetti and his fellow actionistes declaim the Futurist Manifesto, or outside the Théâtre des Champs Elysées in Paris in November 1924, to be turned away from the first night of Francis Picabia and Erik Satie's *Relâche for the Ballet Suedois* (the principal performer was ill), were mostly an informed crowd who expected the unexpected, even the outrageous, from the prominently billed artists. Above all they were willing participants in their roles as audience members, eagerly anticipating that their perceptions would be altered, challenged, provoked. At the multi-media, artist-run Kitchen in New York in the 1970s, regulars included other artists, composers, choreographers, filmmakers and friends, fully prepared to pay close attention to work that might be inordinately slow, or loud, or long. As the mainstream media increasingly covered these intriguing avant-garde develop-

hidden from history: performance art and the imagination

nice relay on L.A

ments, so audiences grew. Two decades later, in London, New York or Berlin, live events by visual artists provide energetic high-points to curatorial strategies designed to make contemporary art accessible to viewers of all ages; within the super-stylish, newly built museums of recent years, close proximity to the artists themselves provides a sense of admittance to the art world, to the rituals and language of its distinct community. At the same time, live art literally brings to life the subtexts inherent in the art exhibited in the museum, in all its multi-media and boundary-blurring forms.

How does the museum curator, the conservateur, preserve this work and find a way to exhibit it as a significant indicator of the aesthetics and polemics of a particular moment in time? While the historian may, in writing about performance art, use the same techniques as those applied to 'reading' the iconography of a painting – a photograph of a performance, in black and white or colour, in situ or staged, speaks volumes about the period and the ethos of a work – the curator must find ways to cobble together documentary material including photographs, notations, posters, recordings, costumes, film, video and journalistic reviews, in such a way as to make this disparate collection of information a visually absorbing exhibition. Along with a creative installation designer, the curator must marshall the interior spaces of a museum and invent powerful new styles of display that can launch the viewer, as in a time machine, into historic periods in the past, while using the bold aesthetics and visual art devices of the present. Large-scale film and video projections, wall-size photographs and sound installations can be used to evoke the social and artistic framework surrounding actions that, while difficult to imagine, are yet critical to understand. Fortunately, the current generation of curators and installation designers have grown up with art that long ago defied the white box (or the black box of film and theatre for that matter), while the institutions in which they work have, over the past few decades, adjusted their arsenal of equipment to include computerised projection stations and sound-proofed bays that separate the senses, as well as advanced lighting and acoustic apparatus that can accommodate such multi-media presentations. Current understanding of the meaning of performance art now matches the means available to exhibit it within museum walls; it takes a vivid curatorial imagination to do so, while holding high the provocative, uncompromising spirit that motivated the live actions in the first place.

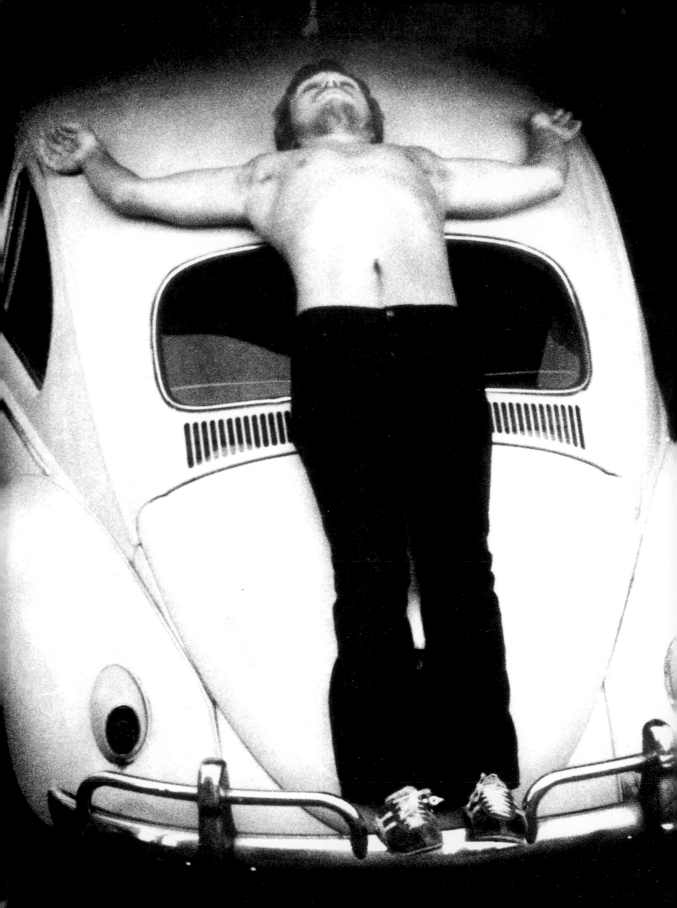

image as icon

image as icon:
recognising the enigma

tracey warr

four contradictory discourses pull in different directions in performance photography: the discourses of the document, the icon, the simulacrum and the live act, and in all four 'truth' is the issue.

Performance photograph as document would have the image perform the role of materialist evidence and proof – showing us exactly what happened so we can 'know' it. Performance photography as icon presents us with a manifestation of the unknowable and an encounter with that manifestation in a state of belief. Performance photograph as simulacrum explores fakery, the performative and representation. The fourth discourse emerges from the conflicting demands placed on performance by theatrical and fine art traditions. The theatrical tradition envisages the live act as primary, cathartic, witnessed and ontological, and any document of it has only a subsidiary status. In the history of fine art, however, representation and simulation have always had an integral role. Add to all the ambivalent status of the body itself as representation and in representation, as both material thing and signifier of immaterial consciousness, and the image of the artist variously as everyman, performed self, and celebrity, and you have a rich, contradictory brew in performance photography.

No art object has a single fixed meaning – each is influenced by the differing contexts in which it is displayed and received. At least, with the traditional art object, there is a fixed referent, subject only to physical deterioration. Performance on the other hand has no fixed referential basis – it continues to exist only through an accumulation of documentation and discourse. The photographic documentation of performance continues a question posed by Marcel Duchamp: where is the art? Is it in the art object or is it in the relationship between a provocation by an artist (painting, photograph, live gesture, document) and an individual viewer? Duchamp argued that there are 'two poles of the creation of art: the artist on the one hand, and on the other the spectator who later becomes the posterity'. The gap between the artist's intentions and his or her realisation is where the spectator gets to co-create the work of art.[1]

Each performance work may have at least three layers of audience: the immediate audience, the audience that experiences the work through its distributed and fragmentary documentation, and the audiences of posterity, doing the same, but adding more layers to the discourses, texts and interpretations of the work. We might add then photographers, editors and writers to Duchamp's inclusion of artists and spectators as co-creators of an artwork.

Gina Pane's *Je* 1972 can only be constructed as a whole work through its documentation (published in *Art & Artists* magazine[2]). Pane stood on an outside first-floor window ledge, clinging to the window frame and looking at a family inside the apartment. During the live event the audience in the street below could only see Pane up there. In the later publication we see three views – the audience's from the street, the artist's through the window and the photographer's of the artist outside the window.

the Live Art moment cannot capture the relationship between audience + art in photo/film

31

1 Marcel Duchamp, 'The Creative Act', in Michel Sanouillet and Elmer Peterson (eds.), *The Writings of Marcel Duchamp*, New York, Da Capo, 1973, p. 138. (Talk given at American Federation of the Arts meeting, Houston, April 1957. Originally published in *ARTnews*, vol. 56, no. 4, Summer 1957.)
2 Effie Stephano, 'Performance of Concern', *Art & Artists*, no. 8, April 1973, pp. 20-7.

Fig. 3
Hans Namuth
Pollock painting c1950s

The photograph as document usually assumes authenticity and authority, yet it is neither objective, necessarily factual nor a complete record. The creativity, selectivity and filter of the photographers and subsequent editors frequently remain invisible. The photograph has a compromised status as evidence and proof. There is plenty that the photograph leaves out (sound, time, space, often the audience). The photograph frames, composes and constructs. Lengthy, complex performances with audience participation are reduced to just one image – the 'good' image from a picture editor's point of view – reproduced over and over in surveys. This is likely to be the most composed image, one that immediately conveys a clear reading: 'giving a different reading as a symbolic portrait rather than as part of a messy and active performance'.[3] Some '60s and '70s performance photography cultivated a deliberately raw aesthetic, resembling crime reportage. Peter Moore, who produced many of the memorable images of Fluxus and other '60s New York performances, described himself as taking a 'truth telling' stance, aiming to 'make the best images he could of exactly what was occurring'.[4] There can be, however, no objective, stable, 'truth' in performance photography. The photograph always thwarts the idea that it can show the complete or 'real' performance to us: 'desire for traditional narrativist closure will always be short-circuited by the limited information available'.[5]

Discussing Namuth's photographs of Jackson Pollock, Fred Orton and Griselda Pollock ask: how far does the photographer document what happened and how far does he or she create the 'documented' phenomenon? Photographs, they argue, produce meanings that are 'contingent on the spectator's interests'.[6] Namuth's photographs of Pollock painting cannot be interpreted simply as historical documents (fig. 3). They are Namuth and Pollock staging Pollock and those images are open to a range of interpretations coloured by the expectations and needs of later commentators, such as Harold Rosenberg in 'The American Action Painters' (1952).[7]

In a 'theatrical' reading of performance an 'actual', live interaction between performer and audience is given priority over the record. The photographer must use available light and silened, unobtrusive cameras. While an aesthetic and theoretical influence from dance, music and theatre was certainly part of the interdisciplinary impetus in '60s performance, in the fine art tradition, far

3 Catherine Grant, 'Private Performances: Editing Performance Photography', *Performance Research,* vol. 7, no. 1, 2002, p. 44.
4 Lynn Zelevansky, 'Is there Life after Performance?', *Flash Art,* no. 105, Dec. 1981-Jan. 1982, p. 39.
5 Kathy O'Dell, *Contract with the Skin,* Minneapolis, University of Minnesota Press, 1998, p. 13.
6 Fred Orton and Griselda Pollock, 'Jackson Pollock, Painting and the Myth of Photography', in idem, *Avant-Gardes and Partisans Reviewed,* Manchester, Manchester University Press, 1996, pp. 165-76. Originally published in *Art History,* vol. 6, no. 1, March 1983.
7 Tracey Warr (ed.), *The Artist's Body,* London, Phaidon, 2000, pp. 193-4, 194, 194-5.

from having a subsidiary or merely documentary status, photography and performance have been an integrated practice, as in Duchamp's performative photographs, including *Tonsure* 1919 and *Rrose c.* 1920s (16). A substantial number of '60s and '70s 'performances' are in fact hybrid performance photography, not performed for live audiences but for the camera. Art magazines such as *Avalanche, Artitudes, Art & Artists* and *Studio International* provided a vital arena for such performance photography.

Catherine Grant points out, in her discussion of Marina Abramovic's *Rhythm 0* 1974, that in looking at the photographic document we are identifying and empathising with the passive, suffering artist's body and are simultaneously put in the positions of sadistic actor and complicit voyeur.[8] A similar complexity

16
Man Ray
*Photograph of Duchamp
as Rrose Sélavy* 1924

8 Grant, 'Private Performances'.

and perplexity occurs in looking at photographs of Chris Burden's *Trans-fixed* 1974 (15). We are forced into a position of imagining the actions and state of mind of the 'friend' who hammered the nails into Burden's hands or tied his hands behind his back before he crawled over glass in *Through the Night Softly* 1974. The photograph has a distance and a detachment at the same time as it allows an empathetic, imaginative entry.

What might be the difference between watching the eye-slitting in Buñuel's film *Un Chien Andalou* 1930 and actually seeing it done? Or of looking at a photograph of Pane climbing a razor-sharp ladder with bare hands and feet in *Escalade* 1971 and actually being in the space with her when she did it? We might still have a gut reaction to a photograph, but we can't intervene. We don't

17
Chris Burden
Trans-fixed (relic) 1974

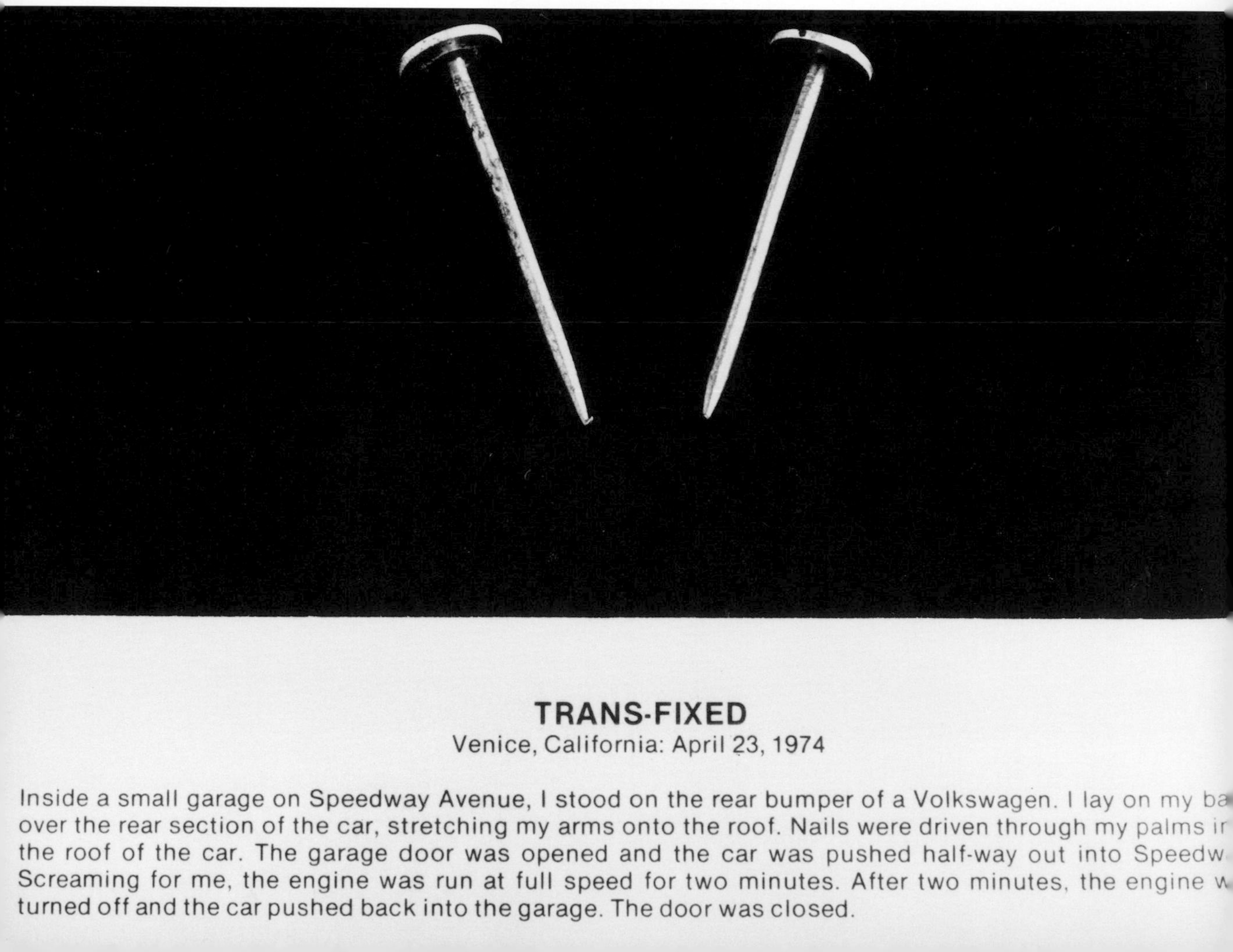

TRANS-FIXED

Venice, California: April 23, 1974

Inside a small garage on Speedway Avenue, I stood on the rear bumper of a Volkswagen. I lay on my ba
over the rear section of the car, stretching my arms onto the roof. Nails were driven through my palms ir
the roof of the car. The garage door was opened and the car was pushed half-way out into Speedw
Screaming for me, the engine was run at full speed for two minutes. After two minutes, the engine w
turned off and the car pushed back into the garage. The door was closed.

have to respond publicly. In live performances, people called out 'Don't do it' to Pane as she raised a razor to her face, rescued Abramovic when she passed out, and called a halt to some of Burden's performances. That responsibility for others' actions, what Kathy O'Dell sees as a complicity and a contract between viewer and performer, is absent for the viewer of a document. As a live audience we are more likely to respond with a corporeal response, a reading below and before language, whereas we are already in interpretation mode in looking at a document. We can also believe that what we are looking at might be fictional.

Traditionally an icon was a sacred image of a sacred person. The icon is a distillation of an unknowable, incomprehensible mystery to a visible, tangible manifestation. It is both a reduction of that mystery and capable, through belief, of fully expanding into an encounter with that mystery. The icon makes the intangible and invisible accessible in portable form and therefore creates a market for the priceless and the immaterial. We now use the terms 'icon' and 'iconic' in an expanded, secular sense to mean representations of people who seem to gather into themselves a complex cultural significance (Marilyn Monroe, Princess Diana) – bodying forth all our desires and needs as a power-fetish. The essential ingredients of an icon are that it must be universally familiar ('iconic') and that it must be enigmatic the paradox of the known and forever unknowable. The icon is concerned with belief rather than dispassionate evaluation and evidence. Fakery and scepticism are concomitant with belief. We raise up our contemporary, secular icons and then delight in tearing them down in a continual flux between belief and scepticism.

From the whole field of artists active in any period, a canon emerges of particular artists endorsed through repeated use by curators, editors and critics, exhaustively 'received'. 'Millions of artists create, a few thousand are discussed or accepted by the spectator, and many less again are consecrated by posterity'.[9] An artist's whole oeuvre may be reduced to one or two works which we take to be 'iconic'. With the disappearance of the original source in performance the performance photograph itself takes on the role of icon, whereas for the painting or sculpture there is always an authentic source and then representations. Burden's *Trans-fixed*, in its title and documentation, conjures the discourse of the icon: 'the spectator experiences the phenomenon of

35

9 Duchamp, 'The Creative Act', p. 138.

transmutation; through the change from inert matter into a work of art, an actual transubstantiation has taken place'.[10]

The photograph as icon is compromised and contradictory because it is both indexical (like the Turin Shroud) and documentary, so that it purports to show us something real and actual which in turn compromises its status as a manifestation of an unknowable to be believed. However, the very incompleteness and paucity of photographic documentation enhances its iconic capacity – encouraging the development of legend by giving us enough but nothing too definite.

The photographic document also has an uneasy status between art document and artist's publicity stunt. In the images of Pollock and Joseph Beuys the artist is the icon as much as the artwork. Burden's *Chris Burden Promo* 1976 was a television advert shown on channels in New York and Los Angeles. It had a stereotypical brainwashing visual with names of famous artists (Leonardo da Vinci, Michelangelo) appearing and being enunciated, culminating with Chris Burden and the final credit stating 'Paid for by Chris Burden, artist'.

Burden's comments in interviews suggest a nonchalant attitude to documentation[11] that is belied by the ways in which he sought to control and amplify the legend of his actions, through his self-publications, *Chris Burden, 1971-1973* (1974) and *Chris Burden 1974-1977* (1978), his film compilation *Chris Burden: Documentation of Selected Works 1971-1974*, and his use of television media. Beuys' photographic documentation rarely has a self-contained legible quality. He worked with collaborative documentors such as Caroline Tisdall to provide an exegesis for both performances and performance documents.[12] In Burden's documentation, on the other hand, there is deliberate obfuscation through the cryptic nature of his texts and the explanatory gap between the text and the image, which allows the viewer to co-create an 'excess of meaning'.

Many of Burden's performances and performance photographs work with invisibility. In *Five Day Locker Piece* 1971 and *White Light/White Heat* 1975 he is an invisible presence – inside a locker in the former and out of sight on a high ledge in the latter. In *TV Hijack* 1972 Burden destroyed the tape of the live broad-

10 Ibid., pp. 139-40.
11 See Jan Butterfield, 'Chris Burden: Through the Night Softly', *Arts Magazine*, March 1975, pp. 68-72; Robert Horvitz, 'Chris Burden', *Artsforum*, 14 May 1976, pp. 24-31; Willoughby Sharp and Liza Bear, 'Chris Burden: The Church of Human Energy', *Avalanche*, Fall 1973, pp. 52-61.
12 Caroline Tisdall, 'Beuys: Coyote', *Studio International*, vol. 192, no. 982, July-Aug. 1976, pp. 36-40.

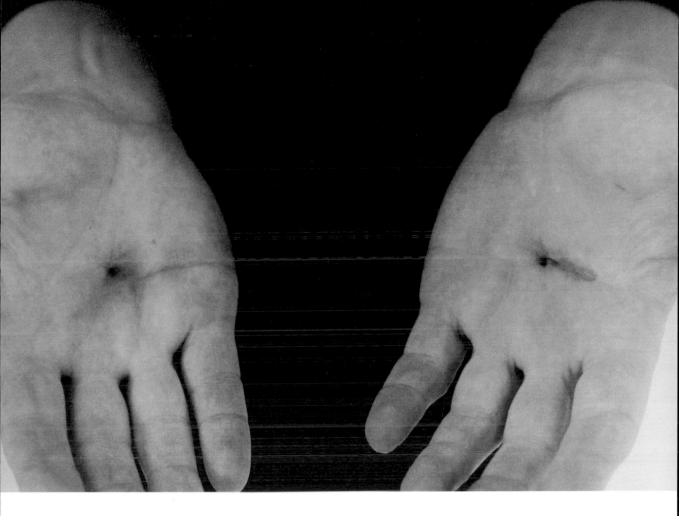

cast as part of the action. In these performances his 'brute presence posited some large and serious conundrum that elided articulation... the dumb body... was a source of frustration',[13] with neither curators nor audiences quite sure whether to interact with Burden as human being or as sculpture.

His works emphasise the point beyond which the experience and consciousness of another person cannot be mediated at all – either live or in photographic record. It can only be empathised with and imagined. Burden's work points out the seen and the unseen in the photographic record and our perpetual hope and failure to find truth and revelation there. Cameras now enter the body, image the brain's activity, show us the body dissected and reconstructed, but still we cannot see what we want to see. The more we interrogate the embodied consciousness with technology the more aware we become of its impenetrability.

18
Chris Burden
Trans-fixed 1974

13 Frazer Ward, 'Chris Burden Transfixed: Between Public and Private', *Collapse*, no. 4, May 1999, p. 15.

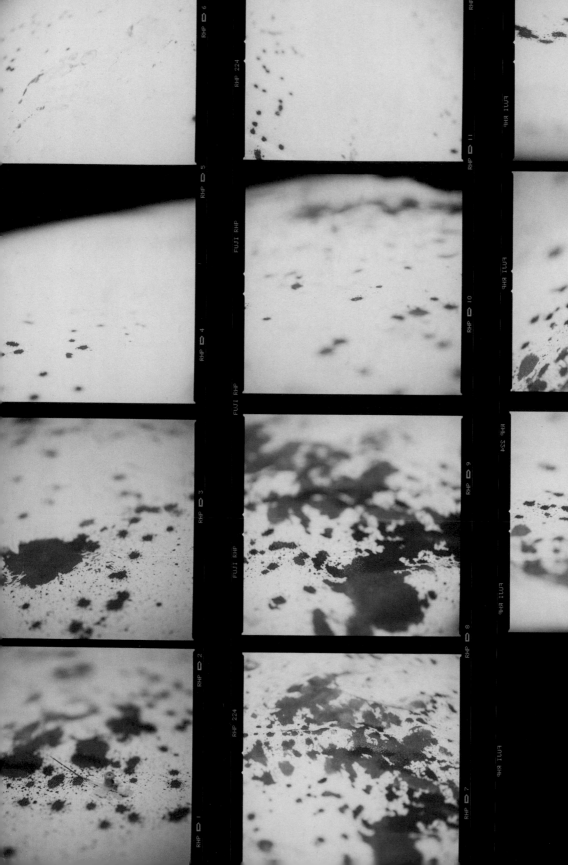

fact or fiction

fact or fiction?

jean-paul martinon

is it really possible to distinguish fact from fiction? This section of the exhibition *Art, Lies and Videotape* appears to present a series of facts: artists cutting or mutilating themselves, leaping into the void, castrating themselves, drawing blood from their bodies. These records of performances are clear enough: we believe what we see. Yet can we really assume we are looking at facts? How can a fact truly be recorded? Two issues contribute to this uncertainty.

The first relates to the archives of these performances. The often inaccurate eyewitness accounts of these events and the vague evidence found in the archival material left by the artists are never quite convincing. For example, even with the publication of Peter Weibel and Valie Export's book on the Viennese actionists in 1970,[1] no one has a truly reliable source of information on Brus, Mühl, Nitsch or Schwarzkogler. The material still consists of an irregular spectrum of facts, half-truths,

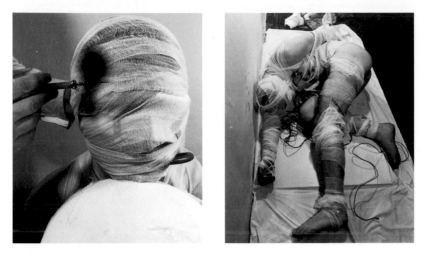

rumours and polemics.[2] The same is true of Yves Klein: we do not even know the date of the leap: 16, 19 or 25 October 1960. Instead of establishing a truth, the archives generate more doubt and uncertainty. The second point relates to the fact that in this exhibition, as in many previous group exhibitions, truth and fiction are shown indiscriminately side by side, with the result of confusing the viewer. In the case of *Art, Lies and Videotape* this is deliberate, but in other cases it may not be, since works are often grouped thematically and not as 'fact' or 'fiction'.

For this reason alone the viewer is led to question the photographs, these ruins of performances: could Franko B's splattered objects be made with stage blood? (19). Could Schwarzkogler have replaced Heinz Cibulka's penis with some

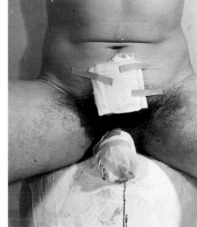

From left:
20 Rudolph Schwarzkogler
2nd Action 1965
21 Rudolph Schwarzkogler
3rd Action 1965
22 Rudolph Schwarzkogler
3rd Action 1965

41

1 See Peter Weibel and Valie Export, *Bildkompendium Wiener Aktionismus und Film*, Frankfurt, Kohlkunstverlag, 1970.
2 See Malcolm Green, Brus, Mühl, Nitsch and Schwarzkogler: *Writings of the Vienna Actionists*, Atlas Archive 7, London, Atlas Press, 1999.

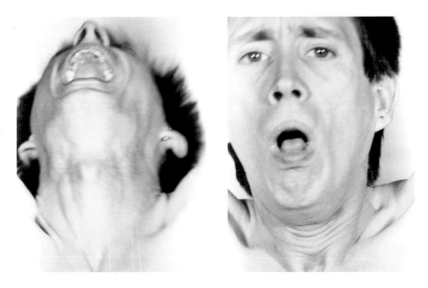

23, 24
Bob Flanagan
and Sheree Rose
The Wall of Pain 1992
(details)

Fig. 4
Franko B
I Miss You (series) 1997
Florence, Italy

3 See E. Badura-Triska and H. Klocher (eds.), *Rudolf Schwarzkogler: Leben und Werk*, Klagenfurt, 1992.
4 See Régis Michel (ed.), *La peinture comme crime*, Paris, Le Louvre, 2001, pp. 252-3.
5 See the film documentary *Sick: The Life and Death of Bob Flanagan, Supermasochist*.
6 See Hayley Newman, *Live Culture*, Tate Modern and Live Art Development Agency, London, 2003.

other phallic object?[3] (22) Did Klein's photographers, Shunk and Kender, alter the image to give the illusion of a suicidal leap?[4] (28) Did Sheree Rose really help the 'longest living survivor' of cystic fibrosis, Bob Flanagan, fight 'pain with pain' in these masochistic images?[5] (23, 24) Can we really trust Hayley Newman? She wants us to believe that she presents us with fictions in order to question the validity of the conventions of performance description from the 1970s; but how can we be sure that in reality she is not, like Bob Flanagan, a super-masochist – Newman having unnecessary dental injections or putting herself at risk of being disposed of like garbage?[6] (29) The question will always remain: even with some historical evidence, can we really decide between fact and fiction and if so, on what grounds?

Deep down, all these photographs ask an identical question: what is an event? How are we to understand that which happens

25
Hayley Newman
Crying Glasses
(An Aid to Melancholia) 1998

here and now, or which happened there and then? This question does not refer to the symbolic contents of the performances, which we can debate endlessly, but to the apparent fact of their 'taking place'.

To announce that all these photographs ask the same question is to assume, firstly, that these artists deliberately presented images as questions, questions for which they knew no one could find answers. Like the iconography of the Virgin Mary, which perpetually questions whether or not the Virgin really was a virgin, these images refuse the certainty of knowledge. They waver between a 'yes' and a 'no' answer to the question, between belief and scientific evidence. The same is true of Franko B's adoption of a pose that has long been commonplace in the religious art of the West (with palms held upwards, fig. 4), which asks the impossible question of the resurrection. In both cases what is at stake here is the mystery of the event. By evading the

44

26
Catherine Opie
Untitled 2000

certainty of knowledge, these images suggest instead that something happened and that we cannot explain it.

This mystery, the essential question behind the symbolism of the image, has the form of a spectre. It is the spectre of a question in the image. These images of performances all put forward the essential, but invisible, question, that of the possibility of the event's occurrence. In an attempt to contextualise the death of Marxism, Jacques Derrida analysed the presence of the spectre in Marx's writing. He understood the notion of the spectre as the 'visibility of the invisible. Invisibility, by its essence, is not seen, which is why it remains... beyond the phenomenon or beyond being. The spectre is... what one imagines, what one thinks one sees and which one projects on an imaginary screen where there is nothing to see.'[7] As the prime cause of belief, the spectre in the image is therefore what makes us waver between certainty and doubt, what reveals itself in the guise of what is hidden.

To attempt to rationalise the spectre in the picture, what haunts it in other words, to try to answer its spectral question – is to kill it, to annihilate the very question in the image. If I say that Klein only leaped onto a large tarpaulin placed over a pile of mattresses or that Schwarzkogler wrapped a sausage in gauze instead of Cibulka's penis, I 'kill' the possibility that the question might be answered differently, that both Klein and Schwarzkogler were mystics and that they really did leap into the void.[8] If I say that Joseph made love to Mary while she was asleep, I discredit the possibility of the virgin birth. By answering the question I kill the spectre, I rationalise the myth, I reject fiction and suppress the possibility of (dis)belief.

However, no one can kill a disembodied spirit easily, no one can prove once and for all that these were only pranks. The Madonna has to be pure to be worthy of worship. Klein's mysticism has to remain irrational in order for it to have value. Flanagan's masochism has to retain the appearance of martyrdom and be characterised by misfortune for it to enter the museum. Even Newman's secular sincerity has to retain the whiff of mystery in order for it to have artistic value: what the viewer sees first is the image, not the label on the wall. This priority of the visual over the written preserves the spectre in the image: the question remains (did this really happen?) until one

7 Jacques Derrida, *Spectres of Marx, The State of the Debt, the Work of Mourning, and the New International*, translated by Peggy Kamuf, London, Routledge, 1994, pp. 100-1.
8 Schwarzkogler is said to have committed suicide by leaping from a window in an attempt to enact Klein's fictional image.

reads the label. Furthermore, many of these artists have deliberately left behind open archives from which scholars and curators are free to 'sex up' dodgy evidence and spin any story that would suit their scholarly or curatorial interests. This openness of the archive also allows the spectre to endure.

The artist's desperate plea to keep the work a mystery, this deliberate focus on the potentially inexplicable, could explain why the events recorded by these images always look like elaborate and carefully orchestrated dramatic spectacles. To create an image that will arrest the viewer's attention, the artist has to come up with a spectacular event: a castration or a mutilation, a sacrifice or a resurrection – in other words something that is utterly remote from daily life and is sensational in the extreme. It is worth noting here that 'spectacle' and 'spectre' share the same etymological root, spectare, 'to behold'. A spectre is an act of revelation. It is a spectacle: something hidden that suddenly and momentarily reveals itself. A spectacle also has a spectral quality. It is an act of revelation: the curtains part and a performance is momentarily revealed. Finally, the spectator, he or she who beholds the event, can also be characterised as having spectral qualities: his or her short existence is an act of revelation between a birth and a death. More prosaically, the coming together of an audience under one roof to attend a performance constitutes in itself a spectacle - a temporary, but revealing, display of people. Thus, on the one hand, behind the spectacle always lies a spectre, and on the other hand, a spectre is always a spectacle. In both cases what is revealed is the fact that something is beheld, that there is an event.

In this game of spectres/spectacles, the issue that really confuses things is the capture of a slice of time by the camera – that is, the re-presentation of the event. Even with modern camera technology, can one truly re-present an event – spectacular or not – in space and time? Contrary to what is commonly believed, I would argue that the photograph does not fetishise the event, the performance or the spectacle as such. It fetishises instead the spectre, the ghost – the question that the artist puts forward and begs to have answered. This process of fetishisation of the spectre is essential for such photographs to acquire and retain a mythological status. There has to be an irrational reverence for and an obsessive devotion to the spectre-question. The lengths to which the artists go to emphasise the importance of the spectre-

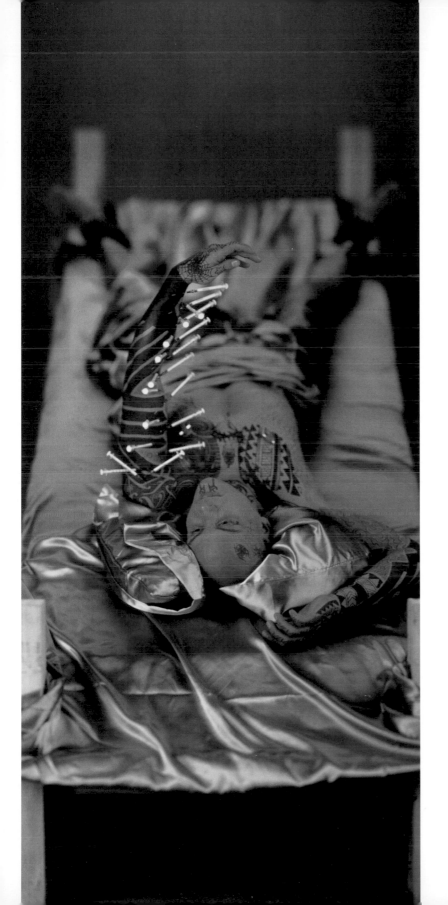

27
Catherine Opie
Untitled 2000

question in the image is enough evidence of this fetishistic process. Their (sado)masochistic performances all seem to ask the same question: can the worst pain really confirm that there is an event, that I am alive? These extreme measures are fetishistic manoeuvres to find an answer to the ultimate question: are we really alive? If I bleed to death, will you notice that I was there?

In a way, perhaps all photographs that fetishise the spectre, that apostrophise the viewer with an unanswerable question, are always calls to the future. They are for the future: the promise of an answer, that a leap into the void is possible, that one day we will understand the virgin birth and the resurrection and that a martyr's soul really is destined for paradise. As Derrida remarked, 'the spectre is the future, it is always to come, it presents itself as that which could come or come back in the future'.[9] Perhaps this explains the enduring appeal of these images: they give us the eternal possibility of imagining the invisible, that which is always to come.

Overall, these extraordinary images, like the iconography of Christianity, push the thinking of art history to its limits: they force us to consider the event of our existence, the event of the spectacle, that of which there is no knowledge, the impossible. In a way, they force us to think (at) the border of thought, an undefined border between historical accuracy and fiction, belief and knowledge, the visible and the invisible: belief that Klein did leap into the void, knowledge that he did land on a pile of mattresses.

To the original question, 'fact or fiction?', I can now put forward a suggested answer: in the case of representation, we can only choose fiction. As the etymology of the words 'spectacle' and 'spectre' has shown, fiction is necessary when one addresses the issue of what cannot be accounted for, that which is spectral and can never be pinned down as being there. Fiction helps us make sense of the spectre behind the spectacle, the question in the image, the event. Without using the mode of fiction, no event can be properly addressed. Indeed, how can an event be represented other than by addressing that which suspends our (dis)belief, that which makes us believe in what is not there – time suspended, the presence of the present, a present captured in a snapshot? Fiction, whether that of novels, films or photographs, allows us to see that which cannot be perceived by the senses alone, that which is constantly shifting, the unanswerable question.

48

9 Derrida, *Spectres of Marx*, p. 39.

28 Harry Shunk
Yves Klein's Leap into the Void
1960

Following pages:
29 Hayley Newman
Lock-Jaw Lecture Series 1998

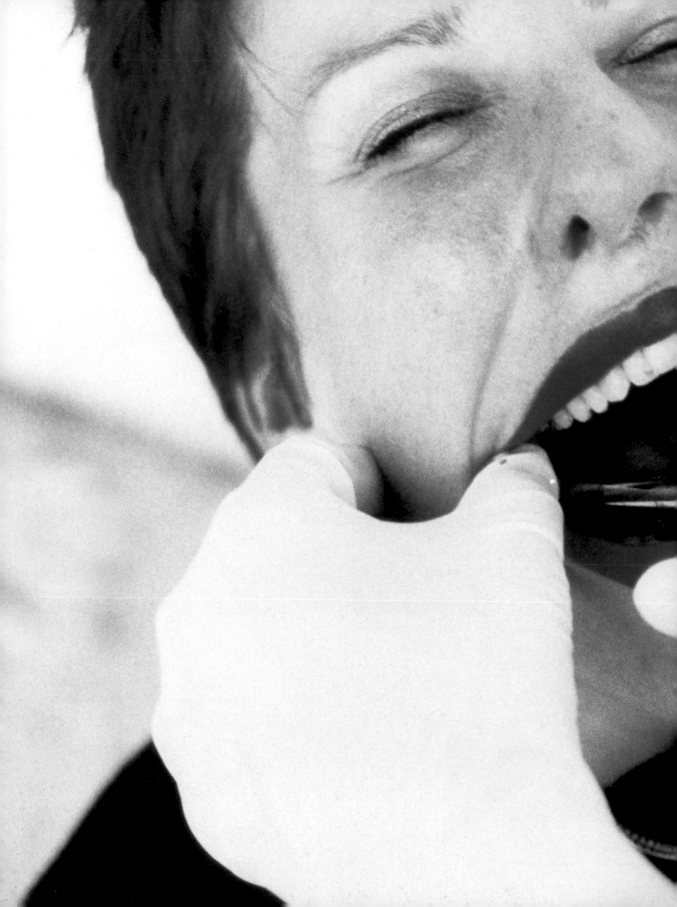

the unconscious performance

30
Dan Graham
Present Continuous Past(s) 1974

performative

art proposes as its 'other' a more complex construct than the traditional audience or viewer. Artistically open to invention, this constructed 'other' intrinsically functions inside or within a performance or an event, rather than experiencing it passively from without. Historically, it is generally considered, performance expanded the frame of art to circumscribe and draw attention to the artist's own actions, presence and subjectivity in the making of a work. It follows, then, that this frame can be expanded to include and acknowledge the active role of all other subjects who, by being present at art's creation of meaning, must form a significant part of it.

It is important that performance is able to do this as part of its (contested) definition. The traditional arts disciplines also entail a performative dimension (the artist's subjectivity and

31
Yves Klein
Still from
Cinematography Archive
1953-62

physical processes, the work's dissemination and reception)
that, although often as complex as the finished, intended 'work',
is nonetheless ignored. By contrast, foregrounding peripheral
enstructuration is intrinsic to performance. Indeed, it is those
transpired inventions/conventions of the traditional arts – the
essentially eventful nature of gallery openings, applying paint to
a canvas, addressing seated audiences, depleting a sculptural
surface and so on – that have provided performance with a rich
seam of material to explore.

For example, a theatre audience may be led along an unfolding
and essentially illustrational sequence of pre-designed effects

the unconscious performance

that (generally speaking) find their objective in the approval signified by applause. In contrast, a performance might wilfully inspire such 'negative' responses as boredom, anger, bafflement, confrontation, unpredictability and so on. Such qualities are in fact often worked with 'materially' in order that the performance's witnesses, addressees, attendants (its 'others') are ultimately compelled to consider their own responses as part of what is being made. Here, a performance – in being designed to blur or elide the agencies of artist and receiver – is free to 'sculpt' responses in ways that expand the bounds of artistic expectation. In this respect it is necessary that the constructed 'others' of a performance be unconscious, to a significant degree, of what is expected of them or of what their actual role within the work might be, in order that their responses be pliable rather than fixed.

Fig. 5
Philip-Lorca diCorcia
Head #23 2001

It is here that 'unconscious performance' might be proposed to occur between subjects – an interaction that surpasses conscious control and by means of which a performative, constructed circumstance is revealed in real time and space. It is arguable that this effect of 'unconscious performance' is impossible to produce without drawing out or emphasising the active presence of the viewer or witness.

One strategy by which this effect may be realised (and which is the specific focus of this essay) is for an artist to incorporate literally unconscious participation into a performance; that is, to make unwitting members of the public 'perform' in some way, or even to make them and their responses the subject of the work. A performance audience, generally, is an indefinite entity with varying degrees of involvement according to the devised circumstances. At one end of the spectrum, an audience arrives at an advertised space at a certain time; at the other end, the performance is entirely unannounced, occurs in a public setting and is experienced by unwitting – even unwilling – witnesses.

In the first case – the announced, or conscious, performance – the challenge may be to create subtle degrees of refraction from

32
Philip-Lorca diCorcia   **57**
Head #8 2001

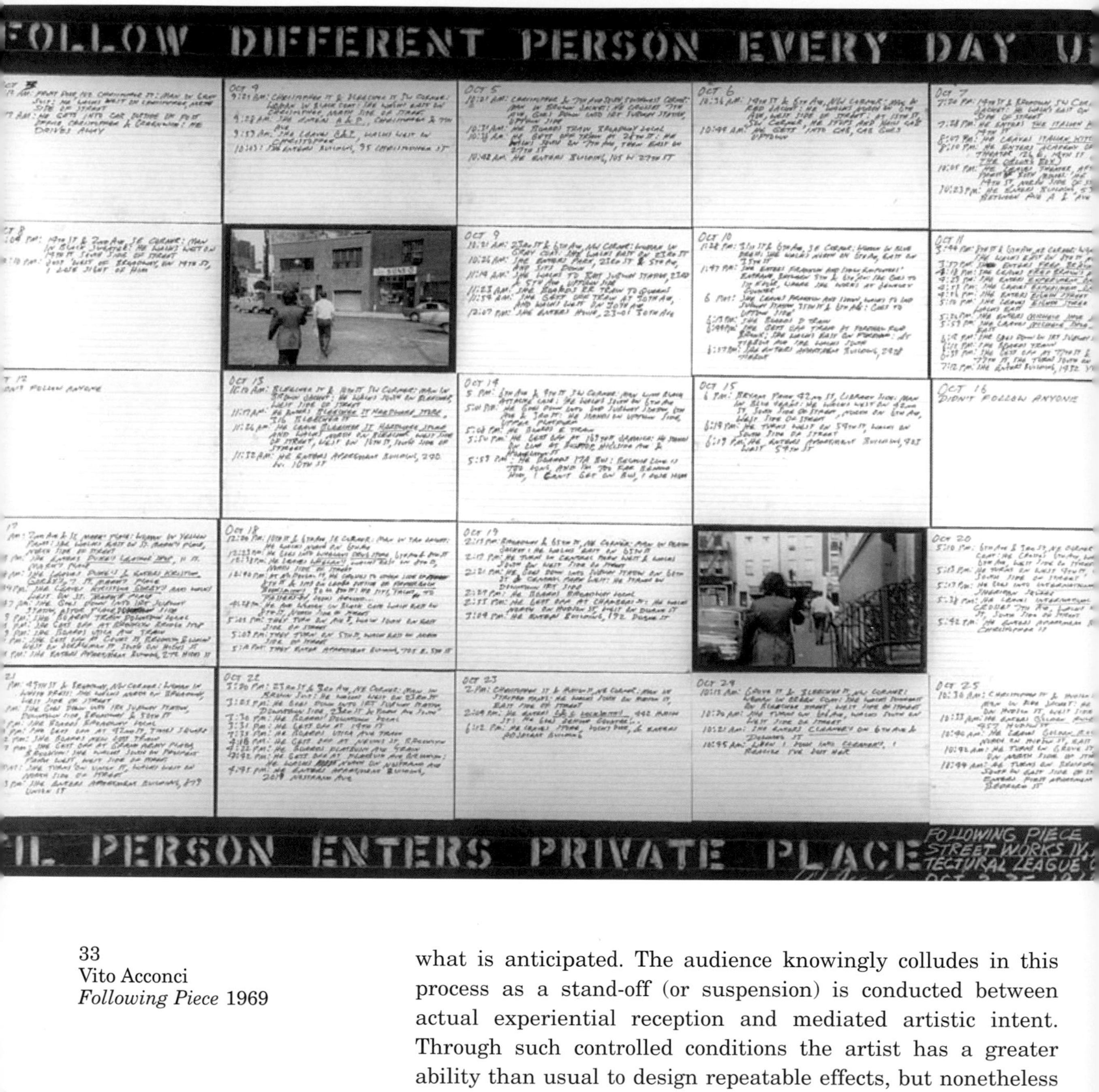

33
Vito Acconci
Following Piece 1969

what is anticipated. The audience knowingly colludes in this process as a stand-off (or suspension) is conducted between actual experiential reception and mediated artistic intent. Through such controlled conditions the artist has a greater ability than usual to design repeatable effects, but nonetheless such performance-to-cognoscenti must suffer from inevitably congealing into generic recognition. Such conscious performance (by which I mean that it is self-announced and received as such) may offer a limited arena insofar as it becomes increasingly impossible to escape encroaching orthodoxy. It is a paradox that performance can never directly be performance in a designated sense, since its consumption by positively inclined spectators creates or reflects a 'fan-base' that ultimately stills the resonance that performance ostensibly attempts to incite.

At the other end of the spectrum – the unannounced or unconscious performance – a public setting (for example) can maximise the capacity for unconscious elements to occur. This may be achieved in two ways. The first, and most direct, method is for the members of the public to be entirely unaware that anything at all is happening. (I return to this example in discussing Vito Acconci's *Following Piece* below.) The second strategy for inducing unconscious performance is to create a circumstance in which something out of the ordinary certainly is happening – there is a recognisable focus for the event – but it has no obvious public context such as street busking or criminal disturbance. Here the question of unconscious performance arises because – at the very least – each member of the public must perform a response.

Although in such situations there will inevitably be many bystanders wilfully ignoring the event, perhaps the invitation to the public to perform or respond unconsciously is equivalent to offering the opportunity to become a voyeur. After all, voyeurism, broadly speaking, might be considered to be the connection of viewing to unconscious drives – an active rather than a passive event – and this is precisely what much performance seeks from its constructed audience. Performance addressed to the 'general public', it might be argued, operates to a significant degree as an exposition of public voyeurism.

A new way to characterise this phenomenon would be to propose that performance be considered as an evolution of artistic perspective. Where paintings, stage events, cinematic or video screenings strive to achieve more than a simple dichotomy between viewer and viewed, performance provides each attendant individual with a position and an experience – a perspective, like that of the voyeur – that is unique.

This perspective might allow us to move beyond the regularly rehearsed argument between the claims of an 'authentic', 'live' event and the mediated, possibly false information of the photo-

the unconscious performance

34
Diane Arbus
Untitled 2 1970-71

60

35
Diane Arbus
*Russian Midget Friends in a
Living Room on 100th Street,
N.Y.C.* 1963

graph or caption that typifies performance's afterlife. Instead, perhaps, we should consider the argument to be one of form, with the multi-perspectival, essentially diffused structure of an actual performance set against its reduction to two dimensions in published accounts. In this sense, the true index of each viewer's living perspective – since we are emphasising real time, space, presence and exchange over mere print consumption – could well be held to be the essentially unconscious, yet active, experience of voyeurism.

The above is a generalised account of how performance might be thought to explore unconsciousness, but if we turn to the works in this exhibition, we find specific variations on the theme. In Vito Acconci's *Following Piece* 1969 (33), it is the artist who functions as voyeur as he follows entirely unwitting members of the public. The audience/performer construct is thus subverted as Acconci watches and documents the actions of his unconscious 'performers' to create his (not their) work of art. *12 Pictures* 1969 also sees Acconci exploring and subverting the performer/audience binary. Here, an assembled 'conscious' audience are seated and expecting to watch Acconci perform for them. He does this by taking twelve photos as he moves in a straight line across the space. The audience thus becomes the subject of this piece and whereas they view Acconci performing the taking of photographs, they themselves unconsciously perform (through posture and expression) their responses.

The question of the 'un/consciousness' of the subject of a photograph comes to the fore in the work of Diane Arbus. Many of her subjects stare directly into the camera, acknowledging themselves to be the subject of an image, and correspondingly Arbus considered her models to be artistic collaborators. This arrangement, however, takes on much more complexity when we consider that Arbus often chose disabled people as her models. Referring to these models in politically naïve terms (even for the time) as 'freaks', her approach to them seems to be baldly objectifying, even fetishistic, and it is impossible to ascertain to what extent she was consciously operating voyeuristically. Like the 'normal' models in other Arbus photos, the disabled models are made 'other' through Arbus's photographic aesthetic (stark black and white, startled looks, and so on), but with the added factor that disability already is politically other. Effectively,

36
Yves Klein
Still from
Cinematography Archive
1953-62

Arbus's intent seems to be to consolidate her subjects' social marginalisation.

However, the interesting question we are left with in relation to images such as *Russian Midget Friends in a Living Room on 100th Street, N.Y.C.* 1963 (35) is to what degree her subjects are unconscious of their deployment within an image that declares itself to be an artwork rather than simply a photographic record. Were Arbus's disabled collaborators conscious of the fetishised, exotic representation the photographer was creating? If so, at that historical juncture, did they consider social visibility of any stripe to be desirable? Perhaps they had some sense that making themselves visible through Arbus's photographs would ultimately provide the means for their physical appearance to confront and subvert normative society?

A similar hall of mirrors surrounding subject/artist/audience can be found in Dan Graham's *Present Continuous Pasts* 1974 (30, 37) – quite literally, as he positioned himself in a mirrored room reflecting the delayed playback of a video recording of himself and his audience in the room eight seconds before. This reflection itself is in turn filmed and played back eight seconds later, and so an intricate, labyrinthine structure of time, reflection, space, presence and agency accrues.

Aside from the philosophical purport of this piece (a comment on the illusory nature of presence and the present, perhaps), it is notable that Graham required his audience to participate in the piece, since their physical location in the work, their unconscious responses and movements, forms its composition as moments in time become 'marked' in the video reflections by the positions of audience members. The time delay of the playback makes it impossible for the audience members to compose themselves or to become overly self-conscious in the way that they might if the video reflection was occurring in the present.

In works such as these by Acconci, Arbus and Graham that foreground the performative as a method, the processes by which the public's unconsciousness is used to contribute to or form the subject of an artwork differ greatly. Other works in the exhibition also adopt contrasting strategies and understandings of what it means to 'perform unconsciously', and this question – given that we all 'perform' our identities and personalities – is an endlessly fruitful one for artistic exploration and experiment. Of course, the process by which the unconscious becomes conscious is historically intrinsic to notions of health, knowledge, wisdom and so on. In this exhibition, as the artists explore the unconscious being performed, we can recognise how, in a variety of different ways, this phenomenon is also a central consideration for art.

37
Dan Graham
Present Continuous Past(s) 1974

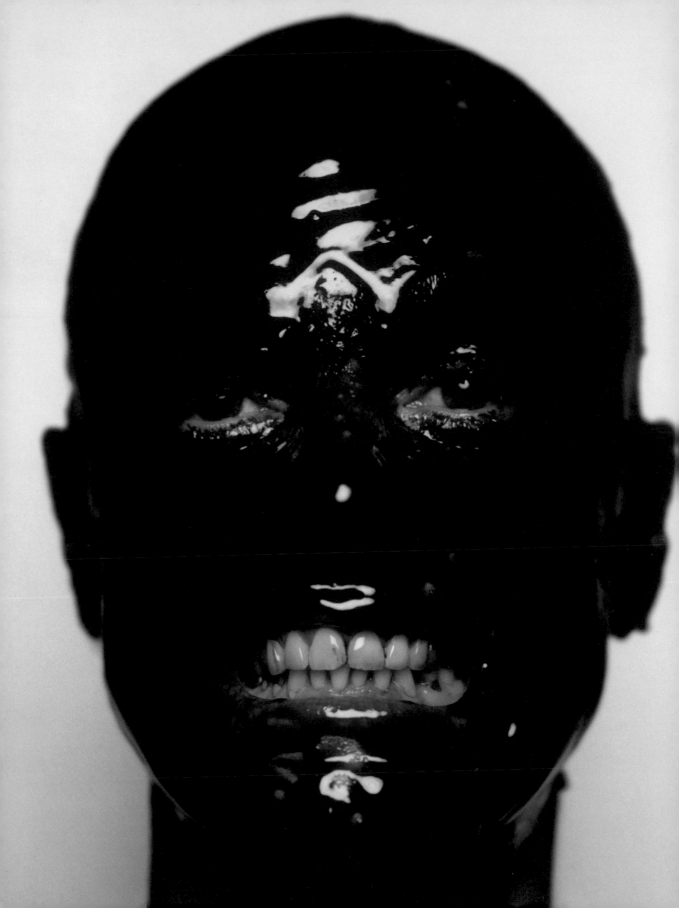

me and my camera (person)

38
Manuel Vason
Ernst Fischer 2000

the delicate art of documenting performance

alice maude-roxby

if you *think of baseball, there's a moment when the batter pulls back the bat and if you can photograph that moment then you've got something about the game. Certain Fluxus pieces have that crucial moment. With other pieces I look at the photograph and remember what the performance was but I wonder what the picture says to people who haven't seen the piece.*

Not everything translates well into still photographs. Performance translates rather more successfully into photography than life does. If I go out to cover a real life event – something happening on the streets – I look around for an image which sums it all up and maybe I find it, maybe I don't, but even if I get a good picture it has much less content than the real event – motion is not there, sound is not there, there's no verbal content. But with performance it's possible that within one photograph it is all there, it's been staged as a full visual image, you can just get it and that's kind of more satisfying than photographing life. The performance is a distillation of a real life event, the act of photographing it distils it even further.

Fluxus photographer Lisa Kahane
in an interview with the author, 2003

Given the current fascination with documentation, why are the photographers of seminal performances largely unknown? Why have they not been engaged in dialogue about their experiences in translating live art into still photographic images? Why do myths

Fig. 6
Franko B
I Miss You (series) 2003
Malmö, Sweden

68

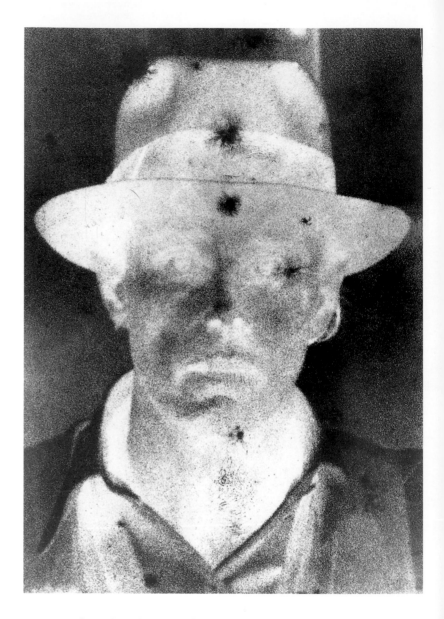

39
Ute Klophaus
Portrait of Joseph Beuys 1970

suggest that the photographs *just happened*; or even uphold the idea that the photographs are *the same as the performance*?

Picture the photographer rushing from a day job to shoot photographs at live art events. Although sometimes compensated, the photographer is more often an unpaid friend of the artist, or an enthusiast hoping for payment if the photographs are published. Fusing attributes from many different photographic conventions, the resulting images show crossovers in style with contemporary

commercial photography, art and film. Think of actions broken down into a sequence of still images: in fashion photography, instructional brochures, cookbook images or do-it-yourself publications. Although frequently not credited for their work, performance photographers are recognisable through their visual signatures – aesthetic idiosyncrasies and varying levels of engagement with the work of the artist. Both the choice of equipment and the particularities of darkroom processes pictorially reinforce the individuality of these 'absent' photographers.

Having exposed the frames, the photographer disappears into the darkroom. Film is routinely 'pushed'[1] to compensate for lighting which may have been 'atmospheric' for the performance, but

40
Gina Pane
Sentimental Action 1973

1 Photographed at a higher ASA setting than the film specifies.

41
Kurt Kren
Still from
Leda and the Swan (7/64)
1964

would be 'poor' in technical photographic terms. In printing their own work, the photographers retrieve under- or overexposed details which might be overlooked by technicians who were not present at the performance. In interviews with these photographers, a picture evolves of *their* presence at these performances.

At his performances, Joseph Beuys was photographed by various 'witness' photographers, enabling him to choose from a pool of images. He preferred photography (which allowed him selective control) to film (which put him into a passive role). Caroline Tisdall describes how Beuys checked that the main elements of an action were present before selecting according to the 'atmosphere' of a photograph.[2] This often led him directly to Ute Klophaus's images (39). Her photographs 'extend' the performance through the impact of her own artistic sensibility. Describing *Action Dead Mouse* 1970, Klophaus writes: 'When I took this photograph I wanted the shadow to look like a body and Beuys himself to look like shadow, hence the emphasis on the shadow which looks at though it were peeling off the wall and window and the disappearance of the ground level: shadows have no feet.'[3]

For Klophaus taking the photograph was only *part* of the process. Different effects were applied to the images given her idiosyncratic use of darkroom techniques. Sometimes she has printed photographs in negative and pushed the contrast to such an extent that the image has broken down into a fog of dots, before tearing down one edge of the paper. The resulting prints look like relics which have only just survived the process of their making.

Fig. 7
Gina Pane
Psyche 1974

2 Caroline Tisdall, interview with the author, 2000.
3 In Victor I. Stoichita, *A Short History of the Shadow*, London, Reaktion Books, 1997, pp. 232–4. *Action Dead Mouse* was Beuys' part of a collaborative performance with Terry Fox entitled Isolation Unit (Düsseldorf 1970).

42, 43
Yvonne Rainer
*Group Hoist
(Continuous Project – Altered
Daily)*
1970

Just as the attributes of a fine arts background are evident in Klophaus's photographs of Beuys, attributes of commercial photography perhaps influenced the extraordinary composition and lighting in the colour photographs of Gina Pane, taken by Françoise Masson. Pane wanted to work with just one, female, photographer. She forbade both audience and press to take images, although the presence of her own photographer often impeded their view. According to Pane this was not detrimental, as the photographer (and her Tungsten™ lights) guided the audience in terms of knowing where to look.

Pane *needed* particular photographs. During the ten years that they worked together (1970-80) she became increasingly explicit in her direction of Masson. Pane required these photographs in order to construct 'constats' or large-format photo-collages as representations of the actions. She never repeated the actions. Some elements included were ultimately out of Pane's control. When she cut herself, she could not know how the blood might flow, so she gave looser instructions. When Pane cut incisions into her eyelids in her 1974 action *Psyche* (fig. 7), Masson was instructed to wait and see whether the blood flowed 'like tears'. *That* would be the image.

Following an action, Masson's work resumed when Pane visited her studio to have her scars photographed. Masson's studio was primarily used for photographing architectural models, which may be why one recognises a particular 'sky' blue in the background of some photographs. Pane was the only performance artist Masson photographed.

In the US there seems to have been less exclusivity about photographing performance. The New York-based photographers

44
Peter Moore
*Joan Jonas
and Babette Mangolte
in Jonas's 'Organic Honey's
Vertical Roll'* 1973

with whom I spoke inevitably mentioned the presence of Peter Moore (and his tripod) as a permanent feature at seminal performances from the 1960s through the '80s. Rather than establishing a way to photograph selected artists, Moore was concerned with building up a photographic record, an overview of the enormous range of performance activity. He and his wife Barbara Moore established an archive of 300,000 photographs of performances taken over 30 years.

Many of the performances Moore documented in the 1970s (of Yvonne Rainer, Trisha Brown and Robert Whitman) were also photographed by renowned filmmaker Babette Mangolte. Both Moore and Mangolte began to photograph performance out of their own interest, as well as their concern that such events were frequently witnessed by only a handful of people. By comparing the activities of Mangolte and Moore, present at the same events but taking very different photographs, it is possible to pose the following question: to what degree is a performance photograph an objective representation?

Imagine you are part of the audience (seated facing the stage) at a performance by Yvonne Rainer. To your right, picture Peter Moore, consciously photographing from the perspective of the audience. He prefers to shoot live, not at rehearsal. His view

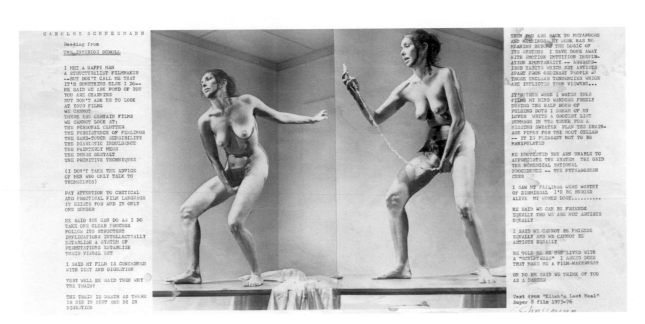

45
Carolee Schneeman
Interior Scroll
1975

cuts diagonally across to the action on the stage, allowing glimpses of the audience. Trying to act as 'neutral observer', he hopes to put reins on his own subjectivity. He wants *simply* to record and avoids trying to extend Rainer's aesthetics and the conceptual basis of the work into the photographs.

While Moore is at your side, Babette Mangolte has positioned herself absolutely in the centre of the space. She photographs the action from a frontal perspective and with a backdrop precisely square to the camera. Having taken photographs at rehearsals, she will have recorded the entire piece at least three times, each time with a different lens. She will photograph 'live' with an in-depth understanding of the work and how it translates into still photographs. Aware of the process of the work, she has mentally broken down the space into 'screen' (to be photographed) and 'off screen' (not to be photographed). As she frames up, she consciously slices off the audience. Engaging purely with the full visual impact of a particular piece, her photographs have an extraordinary sense of space and a coolness which allows for a concentrated examination of the moving body seen in relation to the site. In retrospect she acknowledges what she learned from the individual artists she photographed: fluidity and speed (Trisha Brown), attention to detail (Yvonne Rainer), and how to look (Richard Foreman).[4]

4 See Mangolte's 'My History (The Intractable)', October, vol. 86, Fall 1998, pp. 83–106.

In London I visit the conservation department at Tate Britain to see photographs of Carolee Schneemann. The website reference reads:

Interior Scroll 1975 (45)
Beet juice, urine and coffee on photographic print on paper.
unconfirmed: 1168 x 1695 mm
on paper, print
Lent by the American Fund for the Tate Gallery, courtesy of the American Acquisitions Committee 2003-09-17
L02469

I arrive expecting to see one of two widely published photographs taken by the filmmaker Anthony McCall. *Interior Scroll* 1975 turns out to be neither a photograph nor a 'documentation'. This is photo-collage, a silkscreen print in which two of the McCall photographs (transferred into dots as a half-tone print) are montaged together and flanked by columns of text. The print's crooked edges appear to have been swiped with a Stanley knife, the corners look as if they've been stuck up with Blu-Tack and then ripped down from the studio wall. The 'coolness' of the black and white image is disrupted further by having been splashed with urine, beetroot juice and coffee. Seeing the print in the pristine conservation department presents one with a surreal image in its own right. Test-strips propped up on the conservationist's window identify the rates at which beetroot juice and coffee fade.

46
Manuel Vason
Helena Goldwater 2000

The McCall photographs must be the most published images of female performance. Taken from a perspective in which the camera looks upwards, framing Schneemann in a very angular pose, the scroll from which she is reading loops up as it extends out of her vagina. If you compare McCall's photographs with the blurred and 'atmospheric' photographs taken by Sally Dixon at the second (and final) performance of *Interior Scroll*, you see just how much the aesthetics of a photograph influence how a particular action is read. In McCall's photographs the confrontational nature of Schneemann's gesture is reinforced through sharp focus and harsh lighting. McCall (who was Schneemann's partner) suggests that at the moment of taking the photograph he knew that this would be *the image*.

Contemporary performance photographer Manuel Vason has been developing a strategy to arrive *at the performance image*

Fig. 8
John Cage
Empty Words 1981

through collaboration. Having worked very closely with Franko B photographing his performance *Oh Lover Boy* 2001, they developed a process whereby Vason would start to record before the audience entered the venue, during performance and following the audience's exit: 'I took photographs of Franko B before the public performance so that we could really work together aesthetically ... one was probably taken 30 seconds before opening to the public. As soon as the Polaroid was developed we looked at it and agreed it was a great shot. Then the audience were let in.'[5]

Vason initiated the collaborative performance/photography project *Exposures*,[6] for which he used a large-format Polaroid camera, the tool of his previous profession, fashion photography. Polaroid technology allows photographers to compare the image

5 Manuel Vason, interview with the author, 2003.
6 Manuel Vason, Lois Keidan and Ron Athey, *Exposures*, London, Black Dog Publishing, 2002.

to the action as it takes place in front of their eyes. Selected artists, including La Ribot, Ernst Fischer and Helena Goldwater (2, 38, 46), were invited to devise non-public performances for camera and due to the expense of the film stock were restricted to 10-15 shots per head. The presence of the camera and the expense of the process induced a particular and at times perilous working relationship. In some cases the artist and the photographer examined each individual Polaroid as it emerged, and adapted the making of subsequent images accordingly. The resulting photographs provocatively test out the borders between 'performance photography', 'portraiture' and 'advertising', reflections of the very different ways in which the artists related to Vason.

The importance of the collaborative factor cannot be overemphasised, and has been referred to by many of the artists I've spoken with. Perhaps one of the best known and most successful collaborative relationships was that between musician John Cage and choreographer Merce Cunningham. Cage, Cunningham and director Elliot Caplan worked closely together on the film of the Cunningham dance piece *Points in Space* 1986. Along with the dancers, the camera was choreographed to *move with* the action, giving the audience a unique viewpoint – as if they were one of the dancers. But for many photographers a collaboration with the artist was out of the question and they had to do the best they could. In many cases such images show aspects of the artists' work and process which would otherwise have remained unseen. Jennifer Kotter photographed John Cage in his performance/lecture *Empty Words* 1981.[7] (Fig. 8) Asked why she didn't photograph Cage from a sequence of viewpoints, Kotter says, 'Remember that John Cage *was* God. There was no way I was going to look like I was messing around. I stayed, having positioned myself as close to Him as possible, fixed to the spot.'[8]

7 Kotter has photographed a wide range of performance artists including Eleanor Antin.
8 Jennifer Kotter, interview with the author, 2003.

In preparation for writing this essay it was invaluable to talk with the following individuals who were there when the photographs were taken, positioned either behind, next to or in front of the camera. I would like to thank Lisa Kahane, Jennifer Kotter, Babette Mangolte, Anne Marchand, Françoise Masson, Anthony McCall, Barbara Moore, Carolee Schneemann, Caroline Tisdall and Manuel Vason. The research has been funded by the Arts and Humanities Research Board.

Fig. 9
Robert Whitman
'Jim in mid-air' from *Music* 1973,
performed at the Kitchen, New York
Photography by Babette Mangolte.

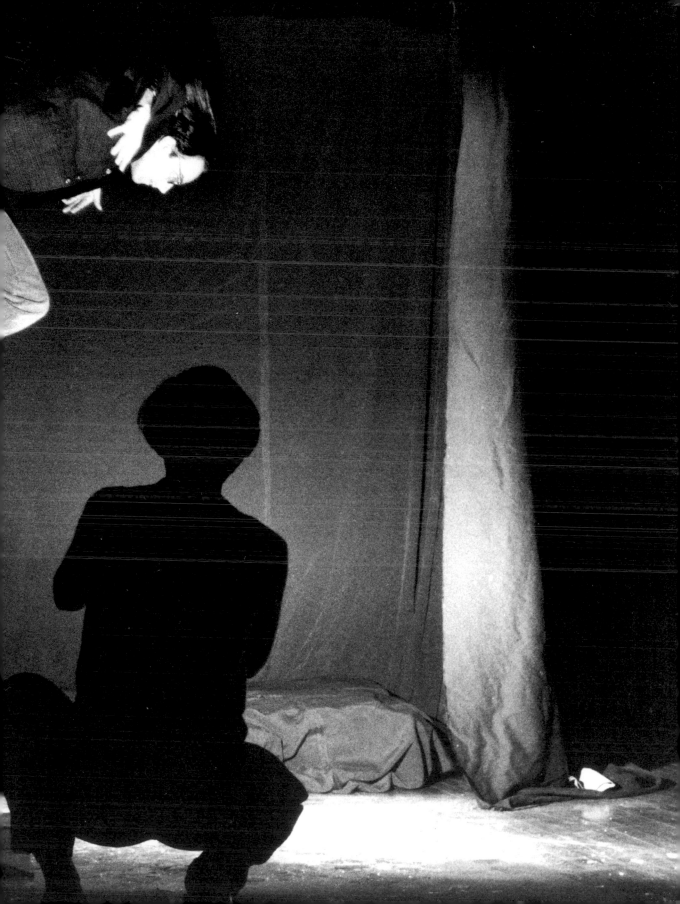

the artist
as director

Dennis Oppenheim
Theme for a Major Hit 1974

the artist
as director

andrew quick

in an era in which artistic practice is increasingly informed by the aesthetics of film and television and the technologies of their production, it should not be surprising that the figure of the 'director' has now come to occupy the contemporary gallery space. The emergence of the artist-director is clearly related to the extraordinary impact of television, film and performance on contemporary culture. As artists have explored these media, they have inevitably engaged with specific practices, in which the director is understood to have the primary creative role. However, we should be wary of embracing this figure, since direction is not only associated with the artist's signature and authorship but also with the processes of command, of control, of order and, finally, with the sources of hierarchy and power. For the director not only stands as the figurehead in artistic creativity, but also as the ultimate authoritarian persona in business and industry. If contemporary art, particularly the works that make up this exhibition, is seen to challenge the ways in which we encounter, consume, remember and document information both inside and outside the gallery space, then an uncritical appropriation of the director might be highly inappropriate. Indeed, as Jean-François Lyotard (a philosopher who has repeatedly championed experimental artistic practice) asserts in his essay 'Acinema', direction (be it cinematic or theatrical) always 'normalises'. According to Lyotard, direction involves the strict controlling of movement and the erasure of all unnecessary or incongruous energies. Lyotard argues that the practices of direction always involve processes of selection, arrangement and exclusion, and that these practices work to construct the 'good forms', the 'good movements', those that permit our easy and untroubled consumption of them. These 'good forms', he writes, imply 'the return of sameness, the folding back of diversity upon an identical unity'.[1]

No-one experiencing the babble of voices, the brutal juxtaposition of images and the playful and moving demands of participation and instruction that make up this section of the exhibition could conclude that he or she has been subjected to an encounter with 'good form'. It would be difficult to argue that these works occupy spaces in which diverse and contradictory energies are channelled to create an order of 'identical unity.' Indeed, many of these pieces appear to exist as a direct response to those forces of manipulation and control that are seen to dominate contemporary experience. This would account for the marionettes, the puppets and mannequins that populate this part of the exhibition. The very stillness of these figures (or at best, their limited and jerky movements) produces an unnerving and contradictory response. It compels us to imagine not only the strange and terrifying forces that could create such instances of inertia and passivity, but also the deracinated voices and gestures that emanate from these motionless puppets. The title of Tony Oursler's *Autochthonous AAAAHHHH* 1995 (49) wittily reminds us that these representations of human forms as mannequins are ancient figures: 'autochthonous' literally refers to the earliest inhabitants of the earth. The exclamation implied by the second word in the title, 'AAAAHHHH', reiterates the fear and frustration induced by our encounter with this brutal reduction of masculinity and femininity to stuffed heads and clichéd gendered clothing. In this work a woman's voice responds loudly to the male's whispered words, creating a narrative that appears

49
Tony Oursler
Autochthonous AΛΛAHHHH 1995

83

1 Jean-François Lyotard, 'Acinema', in A. Benjamin (ed.), *The Lyotard Reader*, Oxford, Blackwell, 1989, p. 172.

to tell the story of an existence that is solely constructed out of fear and isolation. This is a half-story, one that is played out in the imagination of the spectator, informed both by personal experience and by the plethora of domestic dramas that saturate the media landscape.

Oursler's puppet figures give the impression that they are being pinned down by the projected image of the face or parts of the face, such as the mouth or the eye.[2] He frequently deploys and refers to the language of television and film (*System for Dramatic Feedback* 1994), utilising fragments of text or emotional

50
Robert Longo
Untitled 1981

Page 85:
51
Robert Longo
Johnny Mnemonic 1995
Still from film

2 Interestingly, one of these pieces is entitled *Director*, a work made in 1994. For an excellent overview of Oursler's work see T. Oursler and D.M. Rothschild (eds), *Tony Oursler: Introjection: Mid-Career Survey*, Williamstown, MA, Williams College Museum of Art, 2000.

52
Ken Feingold
*Self Portrait as Center
of the Universe* 2001

responses such as weeping (*Crying Doll* 1993) and looping the recordings of voices to create soundscapes that are imbued with the psychological states of paranoia, split personality and breakdown. These works create a disturbing version of human existence that would seem to reflect the inability of the individual to break free from technological manipulation, where subjectivity itself is under attack from the relentless weight of media-driven information and simulated emotion. Robert Longo's *Untitled* 1981 also depicts the human form enduring hidden pressures that appear to throw the body brutally out of control. Taken from *Men in the Cities*, a series of large-scale portraits that included 44 images of men and women dressed in business attire, *Untitled* presents the body as a distorted form, possibly in the throes of pain, anguish or even death itself. Here we witness the frozen image of a man apparently giving himself up to unseen and terrifying forces. There is something prophetic about this image, as it bears an uncanny resemblance to Richard Drew's photographs of people falling from the World Trade Center during the tragic events of 11 September 2001.[3] In *Johnny Mnemonic* 1995 (51) Longo continues his exploration of the destructive effect of information overload through his cinematic adaptation of William Gibson's short story. In this film Longo presents a dystopian world in which information is seen to send half of the earth's population into paralysing paroxysms, thus making corporeal autonomy impossible for a great swathe of humanity. It is a world in which information is depicted as a commodity that can be easily exchanged for individual memory. Downloaded directly into the brain, the excess of information causes the body to spasm violently as subjectivity is seen to surrender itself to economic control. Here the multinational corporations are the directors and puppet-masters.

The puppet figures of Ken Feingold and Dennis Oppenheim are more obviously autobiographical than those of Longo and Oursler, since they are self-portraits or 'surrogates' of the artists themselves. Once again, however, these 'stand-ins' appear to explore the fragility of human subjectivity through a subtle and humorous examination of the artist's function and status in contemporary culture. In Oppenheim's *Theme for a Major Hit* 1974 (48) his puppet alter-ego clumsily dances to a song that repeats the refrain 'It ain't what you make, it's what makes you do it.' Seen alongside works such as *Attempt to Raise Hell* 1974, in

3 See Tom Junod, 'The Falling Man', *The Observer* (review section), 7 September 2003, pp. 1–4.

which the artist-surrogate repeatedly hits its head on a bell, it is possible to read *Theme for a Major Hit* solely as ironic commentary on Oppenheim's departure from Body Art, which coincided with the creation of these pieces.[4] But in the context of this exhibition such an interpretation feels limited. As the words from the song resound in my head, the clarion call for conceptualism and/or psychological motivation begins to feel somewhat disconcerting and pathological. Is this a vision of the artist as song-and-dance entertainer – a figure that has relinquished its autonomy to the unseen manipulators of its strings? In Ken Feingold's *Self Portrait as the Center of the Universe* 2001 (52) his puppet-self peers out from a nest of ventriloquists' dolls to converse with a digital face that floats on the screen before him. In this piece, conversation and interaction are denaturalised through their manipulation by computer software. Words circulate in an endless exchange that is disconnected from living tissue and human contemplation becomes an effect in the interplay of digital information. However, Feingold configures technology to promote improvisation and ambiguity. What we witness are words fighting against the clarity of structure and meaning that would be initiated through the binary code of computer language. Here, it seems, the artwork is capable of enduring the disturbing and liberating operation of thought itself.

4 For an excellent analysis of Oppenheim's work, see Thomas McEvilley, 'The Rightness of Wrongness: Modernism and its Alter-Ego in the Work of Dennis Oppenheim', in A. Heiss (ed.), *Dennis Oppenheim: Selected Works 1967–90*, New York, Harry N. Abrams, 1992, pp. 7–76.

54
Ene-Liis Semper
Oasis
1999

In 'Acinema' Lyotard offers (after Adorno) a vision of pyrotech-nical artistic energy as a counterpoint to the order and the prop-agation of sameness that he claims all representational art pro-duces.[5] According to Lyotard, specific instances of experimenta-tion involve the suspension of what is already known in order that we might become open to the radical uniqueness of the experience (the event) that unfolds before us. Lyotard is not pro-moting forms of creative practice without rules.[6] His require-ment is that art must experiment with rules in order that it might provoke radical considerations of the ways in which we make decisions and imagine our futures. In this sense, art is envisaged as an encounter: one that demands, rather than directs, a response. This claim for an imaginative intervention in the world is explicitly articulated in Yoko Ono's *Imagine Peace Map Room* 2003 (55), where the gallery viewer is invited to stamp 'Imagine Peace' on a series of maps that represent the planet's division into different countries and regions. Drawing on the instruction pieces instigated by John Cage and the Fluxus movement, Ono provokes the gallery visitor to reflect on his or her relationship to local and global political landscapes. The visitor is not only drawn to where she makes her mark but also to the places where the words are thickly piled on top of each other: regions of terrible conflict and devastation. These include locations both near and far away, as people are moved to stamp their hope on the areas in which they live and against the places where conflict is seen to rage at its fiercest.

The activity of artistic intervention, as Ene-Liis Semper's video piece *Oasis* 1999 (54) explores, involves taking risks. These risks might not always be physical, but they do include the letting go of what we already know. To imagine other ways of being in the world necessitates a certain loss of self, a giving up of our identity. The creative act, which includes both the making of art and the encounter with art, as Semper brutally reveals, involves a certain surrendering, even smothering, of subjectiviy. This act,

5 Lyotard, 'Acinema', p. 171.
6 See Jean-François Lyotard, *Peregri-nations, Law, Form, Event*, New York, Columbia University Press, 1988.

as Lyotard reminds us, is not endured in order to direct thought along pre-ordained trajectories, to promote and complete choreographed and scripted movements. It animates the aberrant and unruly condition of thinking itself. This begins to explain why, despite the fact that many of the artists mentioned above have been moved to act as directors in the areas of music video and mainstream cinema, we should be hesitant in our appropriation of this term to define the complexity of their practice. Rather, let us be so bold as to claim these artists as *animators* (from the Latin *animare* – to fill with breath, to bring to life): initiators of movement, action and inspiration.

55
Yoko Ono
Imagine Peace Map Room
2003

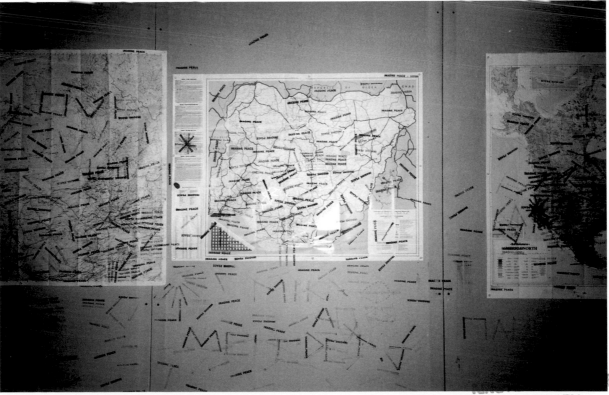

All measurements listed in centimetres, unless otherwise stated.

12 Pictures 1969/2003
Twelve black and white photographs
Each photograph 20.3 x 20.3
Courtesy of the Artist

Following Piece 1969
(Page 58)
Black and white photograph
76.8 x 102.2
Sandra and Stephen Abramson

Untitled 2 1970–71
(Page 60)
Silver gelatin print
50.8 x 40.6

Untitled 5 1970–71
Silver gelatin print
50.8 x 40.6

Russian Midget Friends in a Living Room on 100th Street, N.Y.C. 1963
(Page 60)
Silver gelatin print
50.8 x 40.6

Triplets in their Bedroom, N.J. 1963
Silver gelatin print
50.8 x 40.6
All works courtesy Robert Miller Gallery, New York

I Like America and America Likes Me 1974
(Page 14)
Black and white photograph
Reproduced as a wall graphic
Courtesy of Caroline Tisdall

I Like America and America Likes Me 1974
Film transferred to DVD
Tate and Ursula Block Gallery, Berlin

Three untitled works
From *3 Ton* edition 1973–85
Screenprints and acrylic on PVC
46.1 x 45.8
Tate. Presented by Klaus Anschel in memory of his wife Gerty 1997

Roof Piece 1973
(Page 23)
Film by Babette Mangolte
Films transferred to DVD

Courtesy Trisha Brown and Babette Mangolte

Through the Night Softly 1973
Glass shards under Plexiglas box
15.3 x 23 x 21.7
Collection of the Wexner Center for the Arts, The Ohio State University, Columbus, Ohio
Purchased via the Funds from the National Endowment for the Arts

Through the Night Softly 1973
Film transferred to DVD
Courtesy Electronic Arts Intermix, New York

Trans-fixed 1974
(Page 28; Page 37)
Two black and white photographs and text
c.51.5 x 60.5
Courtesy of the Artist

Trans-fixed 1974
(Page 34)
Two nails, card with title and text, velvet covered cardboard box and Plexiglas case
Each nail 4.5 x 1.1
Collection Jasper Johns

Interval (Entr'acte) 1924
Film transferred to DVD
Centre Georges Pompidou, Paris. Musée National d'Art Moderne/Centre de Création Industrielle

Interval (Entr'acte) 1924
(Page 18)
Film still photograph of Francis Picabia
76.2 x 50.8
bfi Stills, Posters and Designs

Head #8 2001
(Page 57)
Photograph, printed on Fuji Crystal Archive Type C paper

Head #11 2001
Photograph, printed on Fuji Crystal Archive Type C paper

Head #20 2001
Photograph, printed on Fuji Crystal Archive Type C paper

Head #23 2001
(Page 56)
Photograph, printed on Fuji Crystal Archive Type C paper
All works © Philip-Lorca diCorcia courtesy of Pace/MacGill Gallery, New York and Gagosian Gallery, London.

Walkaround Time 1973
(Page 46)
Film transferred to DVD
Choreography by Merce Cunningham
Directed by Charles Atlas
Music and soundtrack by David Behrman: '...*for nearly an hour...*'
Decor supervised by Jasper Johns after Marcel Duchamp's *The Bride Stripped Bare by Her Bachelors, Even*
Dancers: Carolyn Brown, Merce Cunningham, Ulysses Dove, Douglas Dunn, Meg Harper, Susanna Hayman-Chaffey, Chris Komar, Sandra Neels, Chase Robinson, Valda Setterfield.
Cunningham Dance Foundation

Points in Space 1986
Film transferred to DVD
Choreography by Merce Cunningham
Directed by Elliot Caplan and Merce Cunningham
Music by John Cage, *Voiceless Essay*
Set design by Bill Anastasi
Costume design by Dove Bradshaw
Dancers: Helen Barrow, Merce Cunningham, Victoria Finlayson, Alan Good, Catherine Kerr, Chris Komar, David Kulick, Patricia Lent, Karen Radford, Rob Remley, Kristy Santimyer, Kevin Schroder, Robert Swinson, Megan Walker, Susan Quinn Young
A BBC Television Production in association with the Cunningham Foundation, Inc.
Both works courtesy of Cunningham Dance Foundation

Self Portrait as the Center of the Universe 1998–2001
(Page 86)
Silicone, pigments, fibreglass, steel, software, electronics, puppets
Centre head is 'lifesize', other dimensions variable
Courtesy the Artist and Postmasters Gallery, New York

Bob Flanagan and Sheree Rose

The Wall of Pain 1992
(Page 41)
Photographs and hypodermic needles
Each photograph 12.7 x 17.8, overall
dimensions 335.3 x 426.7
Robert J. Shiffler Foundation

Franko B

I Miss You (series) 2003
(Page 38)
Blood-spotted canvas, wrapped
shelving unit with objects
210 x 61 x 30
Courtesy of the Artist

Loïe Fuller

Serpentine Dance (Danse Serpentine)
c. 1900
Attributed to Paul Nadar, Gaumont,
France
Film transferred to DVD
Cinémathèque de la Danse and
Giovanni Lista

Serpentine Dance (Danse Serpentine)
c 1900, Gaumont, France
Film transferred to DVD
Cinémathèque de la Danse and
Giovanni Lista

Untitled 1905
(Pages 8 and 22)
9 irradiated prints
Each print 13.7 x 8.8
Jon and Joanne Hendricks

Dan Graham

Present Continuous Past(s) 1974
(Pages 52 and 63)
Video installation: black and white
camera, black and white monitor,
computer delay, two mirrors
c.244 x 366 x 244 overall
Centre Georges Pompidou, Paris.
Musée National d'Art Moderne/Centre
de Création Industrielle

Isaac Julien

Untitled (Three) 1999
(Page 89)
Series of ten micro piezo prints
38.1 x 66

Three 1996–99
Single screen projection
Dimensions variable
All works courtesy of the Artist and
Victoria Miro Gallery, London

Yves Klein

*Cinematography Archives (Archives
Cinématographiques)* 1953–62
(Pages 56 and 61)
Film transferred to DVD
Centre Georges Pompidou, Paris.
Musée National d'Art Moderne/Centre
de Création Industrielle

Ute Klophaus

*Joseph Beuys in the Action '...and in
us...among us...throughout the country...',
Wuppertal (Joseph Beuys in der Aktion
'...und in uns...unter uns...landunter...',
Wuppertal)* 1965
Black and white photograph
20.5 x 30.7

*Joseph Beuys in the Action 'How to
explain pictures to a dead hare', Düsseldorf (Joseph Beuys in der Aktion
'Wie man dem toten Hasen die Bilder
erklärt', Düsseldorf)* 1965
Black and white photograph
20 x 30

*Joseph Beuys in the Action 'How to
explain pictures to a dead hare'*
(Joseph Beuys in der Aktion 'Wie man
dem toten Hasen die Bilder erklärt',
Düsseldorf) 1965
Black and white photograph
30.2 x 20.6

*Joseph Beuys during rehearsal for the
Action 'Eurasia...', Berlin (Joseph
Beuys bei der Vorbereitung der Aktion
'Eurasia...', Berlin)* 1966
Black and white photograph
19.3 x 29.1

*Joseph Beuys in the Action 'Manresa',
Düsseldorf (Joseph Beuys in der Aktion
'Manresa', Düsseldorf)* 1966
Black and white photograph
29.8 x 20

*Joseph Beuys in the Action 'Main-
stream', Darmstadt (Joseph Beuys in
der Aktion 'Haupstrom', Darmstadt)*
1967
Black and white photograph
30.2 x 20

*Joseph Beuys in the Action 'Celtic',
Edinburgh (Joseph Beuys in der
Aktion 'Celtic', Edinburgh)* 1970
Black and white photograph
20 x 30

*Joseph Beuys in the Action 'Eurasians',
Vienna (Joseph Beuys in der Aktion
'Eurasienstab', Wien)* 1967
Black and white photograph
30 x 19.8

Portrait Joseph Beuys 1970
(Page 68)
Black and white photograph
30.7 x 20.5

*Joseph Beuys in the Action 'Iphi-
genie/Titus Andronicus', Frankfurt
(Joseph Beuys in der Aktion 'Iphi-
genie/Titus Andronicus', Frankfurt)*
1969
Black and white photograph
27.7 x 30.8

*Joseph Beuys in the Action 'Bringing
home' with Anatol Herzfeld, Düssel-
dorf (Joseph Beuys in der Aktion
'Heimholung' von Anatol Herzfeld,
Düsseldorf)* 1973
Black and white photograph
30.9 x 20.8
All works Collection Lothar Schirmer,
Munich

Kurt Kren

Leda with Swan (7/64) 1964
(Leda mit dem Schwann (7/64)) 1964
(Page 70)
Film transferred to DVD

Silver (10/65) 1965
(Silber (10/65)) 1965
Film transferred to DVD

*Material Action: Mühl – Mama and
Papa 6/64* 1964
*(Materialaktion: Mühl – Mama und
Papa 6/64)* 1964
Film transferred to Beta SP PAL

Günter Brus 10/65 1965
Film transferred to Beta SP PAL
All works courtesy of The Lux, London

Robert Longo

Untitled 1981
(Page 84)
Charcoal and pencil on paper
243 x 152
The Holzer Family Collection

Untitled 1981
Charcoal and pencil on paper
243 x 152

93

All measurements listed in centimetres, unless otherwise stated.

Collection Metro Pictures

Johnny Mnemonic 1995
(Page 85)
Film presented on DVD
Courtesy of the Artist and Fox

Babette Mangolte

Trisha Brown's 'Roof Piece' 1973
(Page 23)
Photograph reproduced as a wall graphic
Courtesy of Babette Mangolte and Trisha Brown

Man Ray

Duchamp as Rrose Sélavy c.1920–21
(Page 33)
Silver gelatin print
21.7 x 17.9
Pierre Noel Matisse Collection

Peter Moore

Untitled (Judith Dunn and Robert Morris in Dunn's *Speedlimit*) 1963

Untitled (Morris in Dunn's *Speedlimit*) 1963

Untitled (Robert Morris, *Arizona*) 1963

Untitled (Ay-O 'Floor Event' – Exit Variation I) 1964

Untitled (Ay-O 'Floor Event' – Glass and Porn) 1964

Untitled (Ay-O 'Floor Event' – Written Sign) 1964

Untitled (George Maciunas performing Nam June Paik's *One for Violin Solo*, Fluxhall, New York City) 1964

Untitled (George Maciunas performing Nam June Paik's *One for Violin Solo*, Fluxhall, New York City) 1964

Untitled (George Maciunas performing Nam June Paik's *One for Violin Solo*, Fluxhall, New York City) 1964

Untitled (George Maciunas performing Nam June Paik's *One for Violin Solo*, Fluxhall, New York City) 1964
Untitled (Nam June Paik, Charlotte Moorman and Paik's *Robot K-456*, New York City) 1964

Untitled (Steve Paxton in his *Flat*) 1964

Untitled (Steve Paxton in his *Flat*) 1964

Untitled (Alex Hay in his *Leadville* at NY Theatre Rally) 1965

Untitled (Deborah Hay, *Victory 14*) 1965

Untitled (*Turtles Carrying Flashlights*, part of Robert Rauschenberg's *Spring Training*) 1965

Untitled (Allan Kaprow as 'The Neutron Kid' in the three-day collaborative happening, *Gas*) 1966

Untitled (*Gas*, Southampton Parade) 1966

Untitled (John Cage and David Tudor in Cage's *Variations VIII* from *9 Evenings: Theatre and Engineering*) 1966

Untitled (John Cage and David Tudor in Cage's *Variations VIII* from *9 Evenings: Theatre and Engineering*) 1966

Untitled (Alex Hay, *Grass Field* from *9 Evenings...*) 1966

Untitled (Alex Hay, *Grass Field* from *9 Evenings...*) 1966

Untitled (*Man Walking Down the Side of a Building* by Trisha Brown) 1970

Untitled (Rainer, *Trio A* for the Judson Flag Show) 1970

Untitled (Simone Forti, *Huddle*) 1969

Untitled (Yvonne Rainer, *War*) 1970

Untitled (Charlotte Moorman performing Nam June Paik's *Concerto for TV Cello and Videotapes* and wearing his 'TV Glasses', New York City) 1971

Untitled (*Walking on the Wall* by Trisha Brown at the Whitney Museum) 1971

Untitled (John Lennon and Yoko Ono performing at memorial for Ken Dewey) 1972
(Page 12)

Untitled (John Lennon and Yoko Ono performing at memorial for Ken Dewey) 1972

Untitled (FluxGameFest) 1973

Untitled (FluxGameFest) 1973

Untitled (Joan Jonas with Babette Mangolte) 1973
(Page 72)

Untitled (Nam June Paik dragging violin, 12th Annual New York Avant Garde Festival, Floyd Bennett Field, Gateway National Recreation Area, New York City) 1975
Gelatin silver prints
Each photograph 20.4 x 25.5
All works lent by Sonnabend Gallery, New York

Hayley Newman

Crying Glasses (An Aid to Melancholia) 1998
(Page 43)
Black and white photograph and text panel
40.2 x 50.2

B(in) 1998
Two black and white photographs and text panel
39 x 39

Lock-jaw Lecture Series 1998
(Page 50)
Colour C-type print and text panel
17 x 25.5

Transmartketeering 2002
Four colour prints and text panel
18.5 x 28.5

All Everything 2002
Colour print and text panel
32 x 50
All works courtesy of the Artist

Yoko Ono

Imagine Peace Map Room 2003
(Page 91)
Installation
Dimensions variable
Collection of the Artist

Catherine Opie

Untitled 2000
(Page 44)
Polaroid
275 x 102.5
Courtesy Gorney Bravin & Lee, New York

Untitled 2000
(Page 47)
Polaroid
275 x 102.5
Courtesy of Regen Projects, Los Angeles

Untitled 2000
Polaroid
275 x 102.5
Courtesy of Regen Projects, Los Angeles

Dennis Oppenheim

Theme for a Major Hit 1974
(Page 80)
Soundtrack lyrics: 'It ain't what you make, it's what makes you do it'.
Recorded at Angel Sound, New York in 1974 with: Jim Ballard, vocals; Roger Welch, drums; Bill Beckley, guitar/vocals; Christa Maiwald, vocals; Diego Cortez, electric organ; Connie Beckley, vocals; Dennis Oppenheim, lyrics
Motor-driven marionette, wood, cloth, felt, soundtrack, tape player, external speakers
Installation with 3 figures, motors ceiling-mounted
Dimensions variable
Courtesy of the Artist

Tony Oursler

Autochthonous AAAAHHHH 1995
(Page 83)
Video and mixed media installation
200 x 150 x 150
Tate. Purchased 1996

Gina Pane

Posthumous Action on the Death Control Action (Action Posthume de l'Action 'Death Control') 1974
Two films transferred to DVD
Centre Georges Pompidou, Paris. Musée National d'Art Moderne

Posthumous Action on the Death Control Action (Action Posthume de l'Action 'Death Control') 1974
Two black and white and two colour

photographs
80 x 60
Collection of Anne Marchand

Sentimental Action (Azione Sentimentale) 1973
(Page 69)
Montage of seven colour photographs
120 x 100
Collection of Anne Marchand

Yvonne Rainer

Group Hoist (Continuous Project – Altered Daily) 1970
(Page 42)
Photographed by Peter Moore
Twenty-four slides transferred to computer presentation
Each slide 2.4 x 3.5
Courtesy of the Artist

Robert Rauschenberg with Carolyn Brown and Alex Hay

Pelican 1963
(Page 26)
Film transferred to DVD
Collection of Robert Rauschenberg

Robert Rauschenberg and John Cage

Automobile Tire Print 1953
(Page 21)
Monoprint, ink on twenty sheets of paper mounted on fabric
41.9 x 671.8
San Francisco Museum of Modern Art, San Francisco
Purchased through a gift of Phyllis Wattis

Luigi Russolo

Intonarumori 1913/2003
Reconstructed installation

Awaking of a City (Risveglio di una Città) 1913
Audio recording on CD reconstructed by Mario Abate and Pietro Verardo as the Historical Contemporary Art Archive, Venice Biennial, 1977
From *Futurism & Dada Reviewed 1912–1959* 1988
Courtesy of Eco Italia
and LTM Publishing 2000

Oskar Schlemmer

The Triadic Ballet (Das Triadische Ballett) 1922/1985
Yellow Series (Gelbe Reihe)
Diver (Taucher)

(Pages 21 and 24)
Figure with mask
Wood and papier-mâché, glass, fabrics, rubber balls and Plexiglas balls, coloured
190 x 90 x 90

The Triadic Ballet (Das Triadische Ballett) 1922/1967
Black Series (Schwarze Reihe)
Disc Dancer (Scheibe Figurine: Spirale)
(Page 21)

Figure with helmet
Wood and bronzed papier-mâché, coloured
206 x 80 x 108

The Triadic Ballet (Das Triadische Ballett) 1922/1991
Black Series (Schwarze Reihe)
Spiral (Spirale)
(Page 21)
Figure with spiral hat and cuffs
Wood and papier-mâché, silver and transparent foil, rubber, coloured
200 x 107 x 103
All works courtesy of Bühnen Archiv Oskar Schlemmer, Sammlung C. Raman Schlemmer

The Triadic Ballet 1922/1969
Film transferred to DVD
Courtesy of Bühnen Archiv Oskar Schlemmer, Sammlung C. Raman Schlemmer and Bundesarchiv, Berlin

Carolee Schneemann

Interior Scroll 1975
(Page 73)
Beet juice, urine and coffee on photographic print on paper
116.8 x 169.5
Tate. Lent by the American Fund for the Tate Gallery, courtesy of the American Acquisitions Committee 2003

Rudolf Schwarzkogler

2nd Action 1965
(Page 41)
Black and white photograph on paper
60 x 50
Tate. Purchased 2002

3rd Action 1965
(Page 41)
Black and white photograph
60 x 50
Tate. Purchased 2002

(Page 41)
Black and white photograph
60 x 50
Tate. Purchased 2002

Martin Scorsese
The Big Shave 1967
(Page 16)
Film transferred to DVD
Courtesy Contemporary Films,
London

Ene-Liis Semper
Oasis 1999
(Page 90)
Video installation
Courtesy of the Artist

Bill Shannon
Peripheral Fluctuation 2003
Two channel video installation

Regarding the Fall 2003
(Page 2)
Single channel video
All works courtesy of the Artist

Yves Klein's Leap into the Void (*Yves Klein's saut dans le vide*) 1960
(Cover, frontispiece, page 49)
Silver gelatin print
c.35 x 27.5
Collection of Pamela and Richard Kramlich

Manuel Vason
La Ribot 2000
Colour photograph
101.6 x 76.2

La Ribot 2000
Colour photograph
101.6 x 76.2

Ernst Fischer 2000
(Page 4)
Colour photograph
101.6 x 76.2

Ernst Fischer 2000
(Page 65)
Colour photograph
101.6 x 76.2

Helena Goldwater 2000
(Page 45)
Colour photograph
40.6 x 30.5

Helena Goldwater 2000
Colour photograph
40.6 x 30.5

Helena Goldwater 2000
Colour photograph
40.6 x 30.5

Helena Goldwater 2000
Colour photograph
40.6 x 30.5
All works courtesy of the Artist

associated film programme

Ian Breakwell
9 Jokes 1971
Colour and black & white, silent
Courtesy of the Artist and The Lux,
London

Maya Deren
Study in Choreography for the Camera 1945
Black & white, silent
Choreography and dance: Talley Beatty
Courtesy bfi, London

Dryden Goodwin
Hold 1996
Colour and black & white, without sound
Courtesy of the Artist and The Lux,
London

Joan Jonas
Wind 1968
Black & white, silent
Courtesy Electronic Arts Intermix,
New York

Chantal Michel
...+1+1+1+1+1... 1998
Colour, extract without sound
Courtesy of the Artist

Hans Namuth and Paul Falkenberg
Jackson Pollock 1951
Colour, extract without sound
Courtesy Hans Namuth Studio, New York
Copyright Museum of Modern Art,
New York

Wood & Harrison
6 Boxes (Life Size) 1998
Colour, without sound
Courtesy of the Artists and The Lux,
London

Associated Live Art programme
hosted by the Bluecoat Arts Centre
(in date order):

Frakture: 6th Festival of Improvised Music
13–14 November 2003

Space to Move Performance Sharing
25–26 November 2003

Pacitti Company
Finale
4–6 December 2003

Rebecca Reid
Rhetorical Questions on the Art of Public Speaking
10 December 2003

RoseLee Goldberg

Art historian, critic and curator who pioneered the study of performance art with her seminal book *Performance Art from Futurism to the Present* (first published Thames and Hudson, 1979). A graduate of the Courtauld Institute, she was director of the Royal College of Art Gallery in London and curator at The Kitchen in New York. In 1990 she organised *Six Evenings of Performance* as part of the acclaimed exhibition *High and Low: Modern Art and Popular Culture* at the Museum of Modern Art, New York. Author of *Performance: Live Art Since 1960* (Thames and Hudson, 1998) and Laurie Anderson (Harvey N. Abrams, 2000), Goldberg is a frequent contributor to *Artforum* and other magazines. In 2001–2002 she originated and produced *Logic of the Birds*, a full-length multi-media production by Iranian-born artist Shirin Neshat in collaboration with singer Sussan Deyhim and filmmakers Ghasem Ebrahimian and Shoja Azari, which premiered at the Lincoln Center Festival (2002) and toured to the Walker Art Institute, Minneapolis and Artangel, London. She has lectured extensively at institutions including the Architectural Association in London, the California Institute for the Arts, Yale University, Princeton University and Tate Modern. She has taught at New York University since 1987.

Tracey Warr

Senior Lecturer at Dartington College of Arts. She is the editor of *The Artist's Body* (Phaidon, 2000). Her other publications include catalogue essays and journal articles on James Turrell, Carolee Schneemann, Marina Abramovic, Marcus Coates, Bruce Gilchrist and Jo Joelson, and Heather Ackroyd and Dan Harvey. Her research and writing focuses on performance and site-based art practice. Her recent conference presentations include 'Extremophiles', Arts

Catalyst/Royal Institute (2003); 'Embodied Consciousness and Digital Art', Deluxe (2003); 'Invisible Bodies, Inbetween Time', Arnolfini (2003); 'Marked', Arnolfini (2002); Gina Pane Symposium, John Hansard Gallery (2002); 'A Short History of Performance', Whitechapel (2002); 'Strange and Charmed 2', Gulbenkian/Royal College of Art (2001) and 'Toward a Science of Consciousness', University of Arizona (2000). Her curatorial projects have included OX1 Sound Art Festival, Oxford (2001); *Twilight / Sutemos* at the Centre for Contemporary Arts, Vilnius (1998), and the Edge Biennales (1990–92). She also initiated James Turrell's Northumberland Skyspace. As an independent curator she has worked with a wide range of artists including Abramovic, Turrell, Stelarc, Helen Chadwick, Jane and Louise Wilson, Guillermo Gómez-Peña, Coco Fusco, Jimmie Durham and Cornelia Parker. She is a member of the advisory boards for Spacex Gallery, Exeter; Picture This Moving Image, Bristol; *Performance Research Journal* and *Body, Space and Technology Journal*. She gives regular gallery talks on artists' work at Spacex Gallery and Modern Art Oxford.

Jean-Paul Martinon

Writer, curator and lecturer at Goldsmiths College, London. As a curator, he was one of the founders and the director of Rear Window (1991–98), an independent arts trust which presented a series of exhibitions and conferences in temporary sites across London. Each project presented, outside the conventions of the gallery space (in, around and about different frames, themes, mediums and locations), new or collaborative work by young or established contemporary artists. He has worked with more than 80 artists and writers including Frank Auerbach, Andrew Benjamin, Glenn Brown, Smith/Stewart, George Steiner, Mark Wallinger, Derek Walcott and Catherine Yass.

He has published essays on the work of Joan Key, Jordan Baseman, Lynn MacRitchie, Jacqueline Pennell and others. He is currently Chair of the Board of Trustees of the Showroom Gallery. His research focuses on contemporary artistic and curatorial practices, French modern and contemporary literature and philosophy. He is currently finishing a book entitled *Of Times To Come* which comprises a series of essays on the notions of futurity and ephemerality in modern and contemporary art. His next project is a one-day conference on the relationship between art and the political in the light of recent global changes (April 2004).

Aaron Williamson

Aaron Williamson was born in Derby in 1960 and is profoundly deaf. He studied at Brighton Polytechnic and then completed an MA at the University of Sussex. In 1997 he gained his doctorate in textual and performance theory with a thesis entitled *Physiques of Inscription*. Since that time his work has moved away from literature performance, films and video works. He has exhibited and performed across Europe, North America and Japan and lives and works in London. He was awarded the Helen Chadwick Fellowship in Rome 2002 and the Wheatley Fellowship in Sculpture at Birmingham Institute of Art and Design, University of Central England, 2002–2003. He is currently Lecturer in Fine Art at Birmingham Institute of Art and Design. Publications include *Hearing Things* (Bookworks, 2001) and documentation of performance works can be viewed at the website www.aaronwilliamson.co.uk.

Alice Maude-Roxby

Senior Lecturer in Fine Art (Photography) at Sheffield Hallam University. Her current research into performance photography is funded by the Arts and Humanities Research Board, but began in 1996 while she was Photography Fellow at Winchester School of Art. As part of the research she has contacted the photographers who documented seminal 1970s and 1980s performances to interview them on their experiences and the ways in which they collaborated with or were directed by the artists they photographed. Recent lectures have been given at the Courtauld Institute (2003), the Showroom, Sheffield (2003) and the John Hansard Gallery, Southampton (2002). As part of her AHRB-funded research she is developing collaborative lens-based work with performance artist Lisa Watts, and is also writing a book on the work of photographer Françoise Masson, to be published by Artwords, London in 2004 in a series edited by Sharon Kivland. She has exhibited slide installations and artists books in Germany (where she held a DAAD fellowship), in Scandinavia (Leverhulme Trust fellowship) and in the UK (in the collection of Victoria and Albert Museum, recent exhibitions at England and Co., one-person exhibitions at Tangstation, Berlin and Box, Gothenberg. Her artist book *Lost Properties* was published by and exhibited at England and Co. in June 2003 and exhibited at the Site Gallery, Sheffield in September 2003.

Andrew Quick

Lecturer in Theatre Studies at Lancaster University, having studied at Newcastle, Cardiff and Bristol. He has co-edited *On Memory*, an issue of *Performance Research* (Routledge, 2000), *Time and Value* (Blackwell, 1998) and *Shattered Anatomies* (Arnolfini Live, 1997) and is currently completing a book called *The Event of Performance: Experimentation and the Ethical Encounter*, to be published in late 2003. He has written extensively on contemporary performance and has published across in numerous journals. Since 1998 he has been working closely with UK-based performance company imitating the dog and has collaborated on their new productions *Five Miles, Falling* and *January Song*.

First published 2003 by order of the Tate Trustees
by Tate Liverpool, Albert Dock, Liverpool L3 4BB
in association with Tate Publishing, Millbank, London
SW1P 4RG   www.tate.org.uk

on the occasion of the exhibition
Art, Lies and Videotape: Exposing Performance
Tate Liverpool, 15 November 2003–25 January 2004

© Tate 2003

British Library Cataloguing in Publication Data
A catalogue record for this book is available from the
British Library

ISBN 1-85437-525-3

Distributed in the United States and Canada by Harry N.
Abrams, Inc., New York

Library of Congress Cataloging in Publication Data
Library of Congress Control Number: 2003111551

Designed by Piccia Neri
Printed by Synergy Fine Colour Printers, Wirral
Tate Liverpool Production Team: Jemima Pyne, Helen
Tookey and Claire Young

This book is printed on Essential Velvet supplied by
Premier paper, produced by Condat

⊙premierpaper Condat

[Front cover and frontispiece: Harry Shunk *Yves Klein's
Leap into the Void (Yves Klein's saut dans le vide)* 1960
(detail)